OVERCHOICE

Too Much to Choose From, Too Little Time

FIRST EDITION

By CHRISTIAN GILDE AND FREDRICK M. CHILSON

cognella® | PRESS

Bassim Hamadeh, CEO and Publisher
Kassie Graves, Director of Acquisitions
Jamie Giganti, Senior Managing Editor
Jess Estrella, Senior Graphic Designer
Sean Adams, Project Editor

First published in the United States of America in 2017 by Cognella, Inc.

ISBN: 978-1-51655-539-0

cognella® | PRESS

CONTENTS

About the Authors

Hélène Cherrier. Hélène Cherrier completed her PhD at the University of Arkansas on dispossession and identity work in the context of downshifting. Hélène's research focuses on bringing about a more sustainable and just society. Her current research interests consider waste value, social and environmental activism, and object-subject relations. These approaches follow traditions of work in consumer culture theory and material culture studies and involve qualitative inquiries. Hélène has published her work in quality refereed academic journals including the *Journal of Business Research*, the *European Journal of Marketing*, the *Journal of Public Policy & Marketing*, the *Journal of Marketing Management*, and contributed to Harrison, Newholm, and Shaw's edited book, *The Ethical Consumer*. She also co-edited a book on the theories and practices of simple living. Hélène is currently an Associate Professor at the Royal Melbourne Institute of Technology and director of the Business Honours Program.

Fredrick M. Chilson. After ten years of working in the private sector for a multimillion dollar company as an operations manager, Fredrick Chilson decided to enter higher education and pursue his doctorate in education. Fredrick spent some time as an Assistant Professor of Education at Eastern New Mexico University, where he focused on online education and cognitive learning in his coursework and research. He was also at Adams State University in Alamosa, Colorado, where he taught in the Human Performance Department and focused specifically on athletic administration and coaching pedagogy. Currently, Fredrick is a Professor of Business at the University of Montana Western, Chair of the Business and Technology Department, and Vice Chair of the IACBE Board of Directors. Fredrick has published his work in numerous journals and has presented at both business and education-related conferences. He is also involved with multiple journals and is a managing editor of the *Journal for Excellence in Business Education.*

Christian Gilde. Christian Gilde is an Associate Professor of Business in the Business and Technology Department at the University of Montana Western. Christian received his PhD from the University of Bath and his MA from Boston College. He conducts research in the areas of consumer culture, consumer psychology, and leadership. His previous research resulted into a book on higher education. His teaching interests include marketing, consumer behavior, management, and leadership. Christian serves as a reviewer for journals such as the *Journal of Consumer Behaviour* and the *Southwest Teaching and Learning Journal.*

Lauren Gurrieri. Lauren Gurrieri is a Senior Lecturer in Marketing at the Royal Melbourne Institute of Technology in Australia. Her research focuses on the sociocultural aspects of consumption and issues at the nexus of marketing and society. Lauren received her PhD from the University of Melbourne. She is a qualitative researcher who specializes in visual and interpretive methods. Lauren's work has been published in leading business journals, such as the *Journal of Business Research, European Journal of Marketing,* and *Journal of Macromarketing.*

Erik E. Guzik. Erik Guzik is an Associate Professor of Economics in the Department of Business and Technology at the University of Montana Western. Erik received his PhD in Economics from the University of Massachusetts Amherst. His current research centers on the micro-foundations of creativity and software-based problem solving methodologies. Erik is the executive director of the non-profit Virtual Problem Solving Program, and co-founder and CEO of Vast Learning Systems. For his latest research into cloud-based learning to promote problem-solving in the classroom, he received the 2011 Creative Oklahoma Great Inspirations Award, *The Journal Record's* 2012 Creativity Award, and Hewlett Packard's 2012 Catalyst Showcase People's Choice Award.

Erin O'Neill-Armendarez. Erin O'Neill-Armendarez received her PhD in English from the University of Louisiana at Lafayette, and her MA and BA degrees in English from the University of Minnesota at Mankato. Her teaching and administrative experience includes positions at the University of New Orleans, Louisiana State University at Alexandria, Abraham Baldwin Agricultural College, Eastern New Mexico University, the University of Arkansas at Monticello, NMSU–Carlsbad, and NMSU–Alamogordo. Erin serves as New Mexico's higher education policy analyst for the National Council of Teachers of English. Currently, she serves on the Two-Year College English Association's executive committee, representing the southwestern region. In addition, Erin is the founder of *Aji*, an online magazine for the humanities. She has published a number of book reviews, articles, chapters, poems, short stories, and blog postings over the course of her career.

Stefano Pace. Stefano Pace is an Associate Professor in consumer behaviour and marketing at KEDGE Business School in France. He obtained his PhD in Business Administration and Management at Bocconi University in Milan, Italy, where he has been the director of the Master's program in Marketing and Communication, and where he teaches courses in consumer behaviour. He has been a visiting PhD student at the Wharton School's Sol C. Snider Center, and a visiting scholar at both the University of Bath's School of Management and Karlstad University's Service Research Center. His research focuses mainly on consumer culture theory and addresses the socio-cultural factors affecting consumer behaviour in online and offline domains. He is a member of the editorial board of journals such as *Industrial Marketing Management*, and is an associate editor of the *Journal of Innovation Management*. His publications include articles in international peer-reviewed journals such as *Organization, Journal of Business Ethics, Marketing Theory, Marketing Letters, International Marketing Review, European Journal of Marketing,* and *Group Decision and Negotiation*.

Tyler Seacrest. Tyler Seacrest attained his PhD in Mathematics from the University of Nebraska–Lincoln and his BA in Mathematics from Harvey Mudd College. He has taught at the University of Montana Western since 2011 and enjoys working with students at all levels. For freshman and sophomore courses, he uses hands-on activities to make mathematics more concrete, and he is interested in making mathematics research accessible to students in their junior and senior years. His research interests include discrete mathematics, and especially graph theory—a subject with a strong history of undergraduate research.

Eve Spangler. Eve Spangler is a sociologist and associate professor at Boston College. Eve has always positioned her work as public sociology at the intersection of social justice and social science. Most of her recent work has focused on violations of human rights in the Israeli-Palestinian conflict. Her work has been widely quoted and she can be heard on NPR and blog radio. Earlier in her career, she studied the fate of blue-collar college graduates, the experiences of women in law school, and the reorganization of professional work. Eve spent a decade focusing on worker health and safety, especially in the post-Soviet world of Eastern and Central Europe. However, in the context of social justice, she sometimes branches out in her research to the realm of consumer inequality.

Introduction

Christian Gilde and Fredrick M. Chilson

Imagine a consumer wants to pick out colors for the interior of their new house. With a seemingly infinite number of colors offered by home improvement retailers, and the unique colors of almost every interior designer and architect, the consumer is faced with an abundance of choices. This phenomenon is called overchoice. Similarly, think about people who shop for a new car. A sizable number of different models from companies around the world—not to mention car interior options—leaves the consumer with an overwhelming number of choices. This dilemma of having so many possibilities to choose from is referred to as overchoice.

Overchoice has grown into an epidemic in America and the Western world. Abundance of choice is widely considered as a part of what defines freedom and provides happiness for Americans and people from Western countries. However, when the number of options is overwhelming, the decision-making process can become complicated and emotionally taxing, in turn diminishing the joy a consumer receives from a good or service.

Overchoice is a product of modern society. In this modern system, people satisfy their needs through markets other than their own production. Factors that influence and stimulate this phenomenon are over-productivity, globalism, multiculturalism, and consumerism, to name only a few. These contributing factors lead to a reality in which people live in an enormously complicated environment—a setting that creates overchoice. In this environment, people are not only choosing consumer products, they are choosing identities, lifestyles, and how they conduct themselves in their daily lives. This choosing and conducting provides the context in which a marketer creates—for any particular product—a footprint and profile to which people refer. Furthermore, this environment provides a noise, which is a form of the product-plenty people experience. And this overchoice is a challenge that occurs in today's society more than ever before.

Faced with this abundance of decision alternatives, there are a number of tools and mechanisms that consumers can employ to cope with overhoice. People have to become more aware of what goes on around them. People have to recognize the ways in which businesses and certain industries manipulate them. People also have to analyze and be more discerning of what is offered to them. People have to realize that, in many cases, maybe the most plentiful solution might not be the best solution.

Overchoice, this neglected topic of society and consumer culture, has become more timely and prevalent in recent years. When one reads *Overchoice: Too Much to Choose From, Too Little Time*, eventually one will ask the following questions: What is overchoice in the context of consumer culture? What is the psychology behind overchoice? How does the choice-making process factor into this topic? What are some possible solutions to the overchoice dilemma? One will discover that *Overchoice: Too Much to Choose From, Too Little Time* presents a general thread through this topic and a new, more diverse approach to the subject of overchoice.

The first chapter introduces the text and its topics, contextualizes overchoice as more of a psychological theme, and prefaces some tools and mechanism that can be utilized to cope with overchoice. The second chapter establishes—primarily based on Marx, Weber, and Durkheim—the sociological foundations of overchoice and some of the theoretical underpinnings embedded in this societal discussion. The third chapter elaborates on the economic nature of overchoice and the controversy this topic causes in economics, and presents some solutions to this marketplace problem.

Next to the psychological, sociological, and economic nature of overchoice, overchoice can also be encountered in multiple facets of peoples' daily lives. With this in mind, the fourth chapter provides a cursory overview of how consumer culture regards consumer information overload. This chapter synthesizes some of the consumer culture dimensions through which the concept of information overload is examined, and illustrates how different streams of research within consumer culture theory can provide a new understanding for these overload dimensions. The fifth chapter focuses on the consumer disenchantment this excess choice causes. The chapter reveals how the increasing proliferation of consumption choices has changed the landscape of consumption to one characterized by disenchantment.

In this context, the chapter investigates how consumers experience this disenchantment of choice overload as guilt, turmoil, and emptiness.

The sixth chapter concerns itself with the informational complexity overchoice creates. It addresses subtopics such as authenticity, information overchoice, misinformation, and oversimplification in a postmodern era. The seventh chapter expands on the sixth and provides some educational, teaching, and analytical tools for addressing the overchoice dilemma. The final chapter examines overchoice of course offerings at universities and suggests a way to resolve this problem. Technology can be utilized to make the lives of people burdened by this kind of overchoice a little bit easier.

Overall, the following chapters create an overchoice narrative: a conversation that is informed by psychological, sociological, and economic underpinnings, examines the topic in particular contexts, and presents solutions to the overchoice dilemma.

CHAPTER I

Overchoice

Christian Gilde and Fredrick M. Chilson

1.1 Choice

Choices are part of our daily lives. There are choices we have to make in split seconds, and there are choices that we can mull over for weeks. There are small choices that involve routine decision-making, and there are big choices that concern life and-death decisions. Choices can make us better or worse off, and, to a certain extent, can define who we are. Therefore, in the beginning of this chapter, we offer three different choice scenarios to set the stage. Many people have to make or have made these kinds of choices throughout various stages of their lives.

Renting or Buying?

Assume you received an offer for a new job in a large city that has all the modern-day conveniences you want, and you accepted the job. However, now you have to plan the move to this new location. You do not have a place to live yet. There are a number of different ways you can approach this issue. You can elect to rent a place in this city. You can also opt to buy a place since you are aware of the longevity of this new job. You can rent temporarily for the short-term until you have found a nice property to buy. You can also rent temporarily until you have located a permanent place to rent.

In addition to these basic choices, you also have to make some smaller choices about your place. One issue you have to consider is whether you want to reside close to your place of work or to commute. Do you want to live in the city, close to public transportation and other amenities, or in the suburbs which are less crowded and have more green areas? How many bedrooms and bathrooms should your place of residence have? Should the place be furnished or unfurnished? What kind of neighborhood do you want to live in?

These and many other major and minor factors will influence how you make your decision to rent or buy. How you choose is a major influencer for how successful your choice outcome will be. Once you have set certain goals and have defined certain decision criteria, you can gather information. This can be done in a number of ways, such as canvasing your neighborhood of choice for property openings, asking a local friend for recommendations, screening the listings in newspapers, consulting property magazines, browsing classified ad websites (e.g., Craigslist), or hiring a real estate agent. After gathering information, you can assemble a shortlist of locations. This shortlist is called the evoked set, and includes options that meet the choice criteria you defined. Once your shortlist is complete, you can visit these locations, compare their features and benefits, and then make an offer for the best choice on this list. You might not get "the best" option, but you might get "a best" option from this list. After the place is rented or purchased, you can evaluate whether you have made the right decision or have any regrets.

Retirement Planning

Around a decade ago, the director of a retirement research center of a large mutual fund company in the United States contacted Sheena Iyengar (2010), a consumer psychologist at Columbia University. The director reported that an analysis of the retirement investment decisions of over 900,000 employees generated some interesting results: participation in 401(k) plans had been consistently declining over the years and had dropped to around 70%, while the number of funds in the average plan had been consistently increasing.

Interested in studying the details of this development, Iyengar and her co-researchers examined the investment records of these employees. The number of retirement investment options offered to each employee ranged from approximately 2 to 60 (Iyengar, Jiang, & Huberman, 2004). The study found that as the number of investment options increased, the rate of participation in the retirement plan decreased. For instance, offering 4 funds resulted in a 75% participation rate, whereas offering 59 funds dropped the participation rate to 60%. In the context of this study, the researchers observed that when decision-deferment is possible, overchoice can cause some customers to elect not to participate in the plan at all (Iyengar, Jiang, & Huberman, 2004).

This research demonstrates that, for certain products, as the variety and complexity of the product increase, the number of people willing to purchase the product might decrease. In the case of the retirement investment plans, under the new plan, employees were faced with too many options which added to the complexity of the financial product, thus, participation declined.

Do-Not-Resuscitate Orders

Choices can become complex when it comes to health decisions. Nowadays, many doctors try to involve the patient in the treatment decision rather than using the "Doctor knows best" approach from yesteryear, in which patients just follow the doctor's orders. This more consultation-like approach comes in the face of increased choices for drugs and more health education for the general public. However, certain areas of medicine still require full patient responsibility, such as putting a "do not resuscitate" (DNR) order in place. A DNR order is a legally binding written order to withhold cardiopulmonary resuscitation or advanced cardiac life support in the event that the patient's heart stops or the patient stops breathing.

A variety of religious, medical, social, or familial factors can influence the choice to issue a DNR order. For instance, some religious belief systems might not support the continuation of life through artificial means such as medical machinery. Patients might already be in excruciating pain due to terminal illnesses and do not want to prolong this pain. Some people simply do not want to be a burden on the medical system. Whatever the reason, this particular choice is very involved.

Life-and-death choices are often not easy to make and require some information-gathering and contemplation in order to make the right choice. Of course, one could also choose to relinquish this decision-making to someone else.

****

These examples show that we are faced with many choices that we have to make on a daily basis. But how can we best take advantage of the power of choice options? How much control do we have over our choices? What are the mechanisms that enable choice? These and other questions will inform our discussions of choice and overchoice in the upcoming paragraphs. In this respect, when we can choose, we have some control over ourselves and our environment. A person's need for control (or for the perception of control) over choices can go so far that it can obscure the benefit that is derived from actually choosing something. Having control over choices also influences the relationship between the choice and the uncertainty this choice has—what is possible is also uncertain (Schwartz, 2004). To a certain extent, the concept of choice is so exciting because it entails uncertainty and, possibly, an unlimited number of outcomes.

One example of varying choice control is the ability to choose in different religions. Religious systems can be very progressive or very controlling when it comes to choice areas such as marriage, eating, and material possessions. Religions also use different approaches when it comes to choosing what is best for a person compared to choosing what is best for the greater community. Another example of control in different cultures comes from a study in which Asian-American and Anglo-American children were asked to undertake different problem-solving tasks. The study revealed that Asian-American children did much better when they believed they were following their mothers' orders, whereas the Anglo-American children did much better on tasks when they believed they could choose for themselves (Iyengar & Lepper, 1999). Thus, in general, individualist cultures think about choice control in a more me-centered manner, whereas collectivist cultures think about choice control in a more holistic manner.

Another prime example of choice control, or the lack thereof, is the marshmallow experiment. In the 1960s and 1970s, psychologist Walter Mischel (1972) conducted his first studies to explore how people resist temptation. The marshmallow experiment is one replication of Mischel's later studies on gratification deference. During the marshmallow experiment, children between the ages of four and five are led into a room with a two-way mirror and a table and a chair. The research assistant places a marshmallow onto a plate and provides instructions to the child along the lines of: "Here is what you can do. You can have one marshmallow right now. Or, if you wait until I come back, you can have two marshmallows." Most of the young children are tormented by the fact that they have to control themselves and wait for the assistant to return in order to get a second marshmallow, and choose to eat the single marshmallow before the assistant returns. As seen from the previous examples, the control related to choice is different in different situations and different cultures.

When talking about the control people have or do not have over choices, one also has to talk about the freedom that comes with choices. In his book *Escape from Freedom* (1941), social theorist Erich Fromm distinguished between two kinds of freedom which can be applied to the realm of choice: the "freedom from" the rules and restrictions a person experiences, and the "freedom to" do something. For example, when apartheid was abolished in South Africa, many black South Africans were "free from" certain social and governmental apartheid constraints, but they still could not do everything they wanted due to financial constraints; they were not "free to" take full advantage of all the new opportunities (choices) they had. While more freedom of choice can be beneficial, it can also place certain pressures on a decision-maker. As sociologist Nikolas Rose (1999) discovers in his book *Powers of Freedom*: "Modern individuals are not merely 'free to choose,' but obliged to be free, to understand and enact their lives in terms of choice . . . Their choices are seen as realizations of the attributes of the choosing person . . . and reflect back upon the person who has made the choice" (p. 87). Therefore, a decision maker often makes choices that are in line with the decision maker's persona. And, in return, it might be that the choices a decision maker makes are a reflection of the choosing individual (e.g., values, goals, personality). In this respect, choice also contributes, to a certain extent, to the formation of a decision-maker's identity. As Iyengar (2010) suggests: "If I am this, then I should choose that; if I choose that, then I must be this" (p. 109). Therefore, people choose certain things which define them and are (somewhat) an extension of themselves.

Many situations in our daily lives are related to choices. We frequently encounter multiple options that pin us into a corner or pose a dilemma for us. In his book

Social Limits to Growth, Fred Hirsch (1976) describes these situations as presenting a tyranny of small decisions. This tyranny or torment became visible when my wife and I (Christian Gilde) went out for dinner to a restaurant. We were both looking forward to going to this establishment, as this particular restaurant is known for its great variety of main courses and delicious cakes. When we sat down and started looking at the menu, we realized that it was quite extensive. As a matter of fact, this restaurant prides itself in having more than 250 eatable menu items. There were more than twenty pages in the menu filled with a wide range of main course options, everything from steak to Italian cuisine to seafood. The choices seemed to be endless. The same dilemma happened when we attempted to order one of the restaurant's famous desserts. The menu listed a variety of specialty desserts, ice cream delights, and more than forty different cakes. So, what did my wife and I actually order? I ordered chicken pasta and she ordered a salad. These are our normal default options. In the case of the dessert, the situation was similar. Seemingly overwhelmed by the restaurant's many cake flavors and toppings, we ended up ordering a plain carrot cake. Why do we fall back onto our default options? In general, if I think about my brain, it does not really handle too many choices well and does not want to work too hard.

When studying overchoice, one must examine how people choose. People usually try to evaluate all possible options and then choose the best option. The part of the brain that is engaged when we choose is the corticostriatal network (Decety & Cacioppo, 2011). This network creates the cognitive connections for people so they can figure out what they want (Decety & Cacioppo, 2011). In general, people make choices with two systems: the automated system and the reflective choice system (Dennett 1997; Thaler & Sunstein, 2008). The automated system—which exists on the unconscious level—is a trained response to a challenge one faces. For instance, many people who hear a fire alarm would proceed to the nearest exit of the building and follow their instinct without reflection or contemplation. Compared to the automated system, the reflective choice system—which exists on the conscious level—allows people to think about their decisions and cope with more complex choices. In the case of the marshmallow experiment discussed earlier, the children who were tempted to eat the one marshmallow right away were experiencing a struggle between their automated and their reflective choice system (Mischel, et al., 1972; Stanovich, 2009). At the end of the day, the decision-maker has to determine whether to use the automated or reflective choice system in order to arrive at the best option. Alternatively, the decision-maker can relinquish the choice to a third party, such as a friend, expert, or computer program.

Another way of choosing is to choose heuristically, or to employ rules of thumb or gut feelings to make choices. For instance, a rule of thumb would be not to buy the first new version of a cellphone that comes to the market since certain quirks of the product might still need to be worked out. Another example is using one's best judgement to buy tickets for an outdoor concert on a specific day although the weather forecast predicted that there would be a fifty percent chance of rain. Iyengar (2010) presents how four of the most common heuristic decision-making processes work:

- The information a person has retained in his or her memory can influence what a person pays attention to and the choice-preferences a person has.
- The way a choice option is presented (framed) can affect how a person understands and responds to an option.
- The connections made between different pieces of information to help understand certain situations can impact the decision-making.
- The strong beliefs a person holds often influence and suppress contrary beliefs that enter into the decision-making.

Typically, people making choices proceed through an incremental process called the choice-making process. This process is frequently used in the fields of psychology, economics, sociology, and business, and explains how people make choices and arrive at decisions. The choicemaking process begins with a stimulus that triggers problem recognition and points to an unmet need or want. The next step is to determine whether additional information is needed to make the decision. Then, the alternatives are evaluated and decision-making rules are established. A decision is then made. The post-decision evaluation is based on an assessment of the outcomes and can lead to satisfaction with or regret over the decision made (cognitive dissonance). Overall, this process makes choosing efficient.

Different versions of the choice- or decision-making process might involve a different number of steps in order to reach a decision. However, the basic steps of having a problem, looking for information, comparing the data gathered, and deciding on one option are the same. In general, people try to select the best option available. Furthermore, depending on the kind of choice, one can assume one or more decision roles in the choice-making process, such as being the person who alerts someone about the need (initiator), influencing the person in their decision (influencer), being the actual person making the decision (decider), dealing with the outcomes of the choice (user), and reflecting on how the choice worked out (evaluator).

In addition, depending on the social importance and monetary value of the choice, a choice maker might operate on varying levels of involvement in the decision-making process. For example, products such as toilet paper, candy, and cleaning supplies might require a low level of choice maker involvement and comparison of choice alternatives. A computer, new furniture, or sport season tickets might demand a more elaborate level of involvement and more time to compare the options. Buying a house, deciding on a health plan, or shopping for a new car will require extensive deliberation and involvement as far as the choice maker is concerned. Therefore, depending on the decision to be made or product to be acquired, a person will be more or less involved in the choice-making process.

The next few paragraphs address another important topic in the realm of choice: human rationality in choice-making and rational choices.

1.2 Human Rationality and Rational Choices

The following example should help contextualize what is generally understood by rational choice and a rational human being. Let us assume that a medium-size producer of chemical products, named ChemTechnol, is confronted with a decision about capacity expansion. The company has recently developed a new multipurpose adhesive for consumer and industrial applications that can even be used in combination with other adhesives. Expanding the existing plant would allow the company to make the adhesive on a small scale. On the contrary, a new factory would be necessary in order to produce large quantities of the adhesive.

The managers of ChemTechnol are uncertain whether to expand the existing plant or build a new plant. In general, the best decision depends on future demand. If the demand for the product is high, expanding the facility will not provide enough capacity to meet the demand, which will result in a loss of profits. If demand is low, and a new factory is built, the over-capacity will decrease noticeably the return on investment. The managers have to predict actual demand for the product in order to arrive at a viable decision.

Using the best information available, the managers of ChemTechnol have estimated the payoffs of the different choices, as shown in Table 1.1. News reaches the company's headquarters that demand for the product over the next three years will be fairly stable and higher than in average years. The following question arises: which option would a rational decision-maker choose?

TABLE 1.1: PAYOFFS FOR THE CHEMTECHNOL COMPANY

	Predicted Future Demand	
Choices	Low Product Demand	High Product Demand
Build New Plant	$50 Million	$350 Million
Expand Existing Plant	$100 Million	$200 Million

Given the encouraging product demand for the next three years, a rational decision-maker would choose the highest possible payoff. The highest payoff is generated by expanding the plant and producing more adhesive and meeting the higher, future demand. In this case, the payoff and profit for ChemTechnol would be $350 million. This is an example of rational decision-making in the field of economics.

As in the ChemTechnol case, people can project the costs and benefits of an action before deciding what to do. In general, rational choice theory explains a person's actions in terms of their mental abilities. A rational choice (action) is one in which the decision-maker chooses the best available action based on his or her preferences (Satz & Ferejohn, 1994). Rational decision-making usually expects that the chooser has the ability to analyze the decision information presented and determine the odds for each option (Satz & Ferejohn, 1994).

Rational choice theory requires the actions of agents to be rational and calculative (Scott, 2000). In the area of rational choice, Weber (1920/1968) built a typology of action which concerns actions in areas such as emotions, affects, and value-orientation, which was later advanced by Parsons (1937). Rational choice theory, to a certain extent, also touches on exchange theory when it is viewed in the context of social interactions (Blau, 1964; Coleman & O'Sullivan, 1990; Homans,

1971). In recent years, rational choice theory has become much more mathematical and computational, and has been employed in consumer analytics, operations management, and behavioral finance. What is similar in all the variants of rational choice theory is that rational action can be explained by individual human actions (Elster, 1989). Rational choice theory also looks at how production, distribution, and consumption are organized, an approach which can be expanded to other fields such as information processing or lifetime value analysis (Scott 2000).

In rational choice theory, it is assumed that individuals are motivated by goals and wants which they exhibit through their preferences (Heath, 1976). Rational choice theory also expects that the decision-makers can guess the outcomes of the decision alternatives they face (information processing), and are able to calculate which one would be the most satisfying alternative for them (calculation) (Heath, 1976). Individuals have to act within certain limitations and with the information they have. Usually, individuals cannot get all the things they want, so they have to make rational choices with their goals and limited resources in mind.

Herbert Simon (1976), the social and behavioral scientist and Nobel Prize winner, proposed that a rational human decision should be efficient and practical to implement with the resources one has. Any rational human decision involves a choice selected from a number of alternatives which focuses on one or more goals. Simon (1976) suggested that options have real outcomes which consist of personal actions or non-actions that are impacted by individual values and factors relating to the surrounding environment. In practice, some of the results may be conscious or unconscious, some of the outcomes may be intended or unintended, and some of the means and ends may not really fit together or completely connect.

The ultimate goal of rational decision-making is to select the alternative that results in the most wanted option over all the offers. In the ChemTechnol example, the best option was to expand the plant and reap the maximum possible payoff of $350 million. This task of selecting an alternative can be divided into three steps (Simon 1955, p.100):

1. The itemizing of all the alternatives that are part of the choice set.
2. The determining of the pay-offs that result from the choices.
3. The ranking of all the pay-offs that are associated with the choices.

It is highly improbable that a person could know all of their options or all of the consequences that result from each of the options. Given the inevitable limitations of rational decision-making, what approach or mechanism can a person or organization employ to achieve the best result? Simon (1976) writes:

> The human being striving for rationality and restricted within the limits of his knowledge has developed some working procedures that partially overcome this difficulty. These procedures consist in assuming that he can isolate from the rest of the world a closed system containing only a limited number of variables and a limited range of consequences. (p. 94)

After establishing some of the fundamentals of choice and looking at how rational decision-makers are described in the context of choice, we now transition to the main concern of this book, which is how people relate to too much choice.

1.3 Overchoice

> The word 'choice' almost always carriers a positive connotation [thus, the more choice, the better]; conversely, to say 'I had little or no choice' is usually to apologize or to explain one's unfortunately limited predicament.
>
> (Iyengar, 2010, p. 179)

Is it always true that too much choice is good? Perhaps not in today's society. Past research on choice, judgment, and decision-making has argued widely for the positive effects of choice; however, most of these studies did not offer, on average, more than seven choice options to participants (Scheibehenne, Greifeneder, & Todd, 2010). In his paper "The Magical Number Seven, Plus or Minus Two: Some Limits on Our Capacity for Processing Information," Miller (1956) finds that too much choice can be confusing, or outright detrimental, to successful decision-making. In one study, Iyengar and Lepper (2000) set up a jam sample table in a gourmet food store. One version of the table had 6 varieties of jam, whereas the other version had

24 varieties of jam. The study revealed that only 3% of the people sampling from the 24 varieties of jams actually purchased a jam, whereas 30% of the consumers sampling from the 6 varieties of jams purchased a jar. Iyengar (2010) finds that "people can handle only five to nine items before they begin to consistently make errors in perception" (Iyengar 2010, p. 182). Shah and Wolford (2007) write about an inverted U-shape on buying that develops as marketers increase the number of options that consumers have available to them for purchase. The study finds that as the number of alternatives increase, the proportion of buying first increases and then decreases, peaking at a number of ten and forming an inverted U-shape.

Thus, in many instances, excess choice might not be advantageous after all. The futurist Alvin Toffler (1970) forecasted that technological changes would result in advances and that the modern-day industrial revolution would result in great abundance of choice. Toffler (1970) suggested that, "Ironically, the people of the future may suffer not from an absence of choice, but from a paralyzing surfeit of it" (p. 264). Supporting this argument are recent data by Grieder that show that the average American supermarket now stocks 20,000 more products than it did 30 years ago (as cited in 5MetaCom, 2007). Whereas in the 1950s, the average grocery store stocked 3,700 products, the average supermarket today offers 45,000 products, and the average Walmart stocks 100,000 products. Even more alternatives are available online. For instance, Amazon.com offers 27 million books, and Match.com offers 15 million dating options (Iyengar & Agrawal, 2010). Alvin Toffler (1970), who popularized the term overchoice, realized that, "There comes a time, in short, when choice turns into overchoice and freedom into un-freedom" (p. 250). Toffler's un-freedom means that there are too many choices to make efficient and satisfying decisions. Toffler mentioned that maximizing individual choice is considered an economic goal primarily in Western societies. In the second half of the twentieth century, consumers had more money to spend to satisfy their unique desires, and as a result, companies began producing additional products. In addition, as technologies matured, it became less and less expensive to increase product variation. Product diversity or heterogeneity (product abundance) replaced past product uniformity or homogeneity (product sameness) (Toffler, 1970).

When talking about overchoice, one has to consider the concepts of choice variety and choice complexity. Variety and complexity differ in their importance to advance through the steps of choice-making, which ultimately result in the purchase decision of the consumer. Variety is the positive aspect of assortment.

When selecting an assortment during the need-recognition stage—the first stage of choice-making process—consumers would like to have more variety (Townsend & Kahn, 2014). However, for large choice sets, the increased perceptions of variety could be associated with increased perceptions of complexity, which can result into a feeling that one is overloaded with choices (Townsend & Kahn, 2014).

Compared to choice variety, choice complexity is the negative aspect of assortment. Complexity is important for the second step in the choice-making process, when a consumer is asked to select an alternative from a set of choices (Townsend & Kahn, 2014). Townsend and Kahn (2014) find that when an individual chooses an item within a choice set, too much variety might increase complexity. This discussion leads to another research finding: as the complexity of making choices grows, people tend to simplify their decision-making processes by employing simple heuristic approaches (Payne, 1982; Payne, Bettman, & Johnson, 1988, 1993; Timmermans, 1993; Wright, 1975). For instance, a comparison of the decision strategies of people presented with three, six, or nine alternatives showed that 21% used an elimination strategy in the case of three options, 31% used an elimination strategy in the case of six options, and 77% used an elimination strategy in the case of nine options (Timmermans, 1993). The increase in the percentage of participants who used an elimination strategy as the number of alternatives increased was linked to a decrease in the percentage of information used. This decrease in the information used as complexity increases suggests that choice overload may trigger an employment of more efficient decision rules.

However, overchoice does not necessarily have to be bad. In his book *The Long Tail,* Chris Anderson (2006) presents a more positive view of overchoice. He finds that, for instance, the millions of books that sell only 100 copies or so can make up a considerable portion of the overall market share of book sales (up to 25%); yet, the few books that sell millions of copies still make up the majority of the market share (up to 75%). When illustrated in a line graph ranked from the highest selling items to the lowest, the beginning of the graph is very tall and thin whereas the rest of the graph is getting slimmer and slimmer and seemingly converging towards zero in a long tail. Therefore, a variety of products can be a profitable addition to the product mix of a business.

In addition, overchoice should not be confusing when one approaches it the right way. If one can order the abundance of choices, place them into the right categories and make sense of them, then one can use this variety to their benefit.

This ordering or categorizing can be made easier by using tools such as internet search options, expert reviews, consumer reports, or prior product knowledge. For instance, a consumer can group a product by price, features, or availability. In order to make variety-of-choice work, in addition to variety, "information about that variety and what other consumers before us have done with the same choices" (Anderson, 2006, p. 174) is needed.

Does more choice result in more sales? Overall, the current research is inconclusive, and lacks solid statistical evidence to support the notion that more choice results in higher sales (Scheibehenne, Greifeneder, & Todd, 2010). However, some research suggests that when choice is meaningful, more choice can improve the likelihood that consumers find what they want (Anderson, 2006). Other related research reveals that consumers selected options more often when these options are offered in combination with many other choices (Brown, Read, & Summers, 2002).

Overchoice originated from more demand for diversity and increased individualism (Toffler, 1970). In addition, the number of available choices also exploded due to more efficient product-distribution networks and increasing globalization. After discussing some of the major aspects of overchoice in the previous paragraphs, the next section focuses on what is at the center of the overchoice paradigm: choice set size.

1.4 Choice Set Size

While the size of the assortment is at the center of overchoice theory, there is no exact definition for what constitutes too much choice. Iyengar and Lepper (2000) described overchoice as a "reasonably large, but not ecologically unusual, number of options" (p. 996). For instance, in studies by Reutskaja (2008) and Reutskaja and Hogarth (2009), the assortment sizes varied between 5 and 30 with increments of 5. In a study by Shah and Wolford (2007), the assortment sizes varied between 2 and 20 with increments of 2.

What passes as a small or large assortment depends on the perception of the consumer and may be shaped by the newness of the product category and the overall developmental stage of the market. For example, in 1990, the average US household had access to 33 television channels, whereas in 2008 the average household had access to 130 television channels (The Nielsen Company, 2009). In this context, it is generally understood that a choice set size greater than 10 can cause problems as far as decision-making efficiency and choosing the best outcome are concerned (Miller, 1956). In addition, one should consider a seemingly basic—yet important—methodological characteristic of prior studies: when surveying more dated literature on the topic, one discovers that in old studies on choice overload the number of options was capped at approximately 6. It is possible that these studies capped the choice options at 6 simple out of convenience.

A review by Scheibehenne, Greifeneder, and Todd (2010) of overchoice research studies using 63 overchoice conditions and 50 experiments reveals that the average size for small choice sets was 7, whereas the average size for large choice sets was 33 (this is to some extent in line with other recent studies). These findings are somewhat similar to the results of a meta-analysis of choice overload by Chernev, Bockenholt, and Goodman (2015). This meta-analysis of choice set sizes across individual studies shows that the average size for a small assortment was 6 options and the average size for a large assortment was 24 options.

Why is choice set size so important when studying overchoice? One explanation is that the variable of set size is at the center of the overchoice paradigm. It defines, to a certain extent, why people either suffer from or enjoy overchoice. For example, too much choice can decrease the motivation to choose and the satisfaction with the chosen option. Current research in consumer psychology and social psychology has demonstrated that when customers do not have a product preference (ideal product) it is easier for them to choose from smaller assortments than from larger assortments (Chernev, 2003a, 2003b; Iyengar & Lepper, 2000; Schwartz, 2000, 2004; Shah & Wolford, 2007). Large assortments seem to overwhelm customers with information, making it more difficult for people to find the product they like. We can infer that a plentitude of goods can cause unwanted economic and psychological costs such as long search times, dissatisfaction, and choice deferral.

Recently, researchers (e.g., Chernev, 2003; Gourville & Soman, 2005; Iyengar & Lepper, 2000; Lehmann, 1998) have found that large assortments can create other negative effects and have discovered factors that influence these undesirable results. For example, consumers might not choose an option impartially that matches their desires from larger assortments because of a lack of access to choice screening-tools (Diehl, Kornish, & Lynch, 2003). Or, consumers might search inefficiently when using these tools (Diehl, 2005). As a matter of fact, consumers might not even perceive options to be better when options stem from a larger assortment (Benartzi & Thaler, 2002). Large sets can also lower the consumer's confidence in having made a good decision (Chernev, 2003). Furthermore, when large sets make consumers uncertain about their preference (Dhar, 1997), or feel overloaded (Iyengar & Lepper, 2000), consumers may postpone their decision-making. Finally, in the face of large assortments, consumers may experience more cognitive dissonance (post-decision regret), even when they made good choices (Gourville & Soman, 2005).

Reutskaja and Hogarth (2009) found that a person's satisfaction with a gift box decreased as the number gift boxes are offered for selection increased, and Haynes (2009) discovered similar results for choices among lottery prices. Similarly, Shah and Wolford (2007) found that the percentage of participants who were motivated to buy a black pen declined from 70% when selecting a pen from small assortments (8 to 14 pens), to 33% when selecting a pen from large assortments (16 to 20 pens).

Overall, this empirical evidence favors the notion that large assortments can have negative consequences. This evidence refutes many theories in the fields of economics, psychology, and management, which assert that more choice makes decision-makers better off. For example, an advantage of excess choice is that it can help someone find the best choice option, or at least a satisfactory choice option. Large assortments make it more likely that different types of consumers find something they need or desire. Having more options is often considered as an important aspect of personal freedom; choice enables individuals to live their lives how they envision them (Schwartz, 2004). Having more options to choose from also makes it easier for consumers to search for and compare different options (Hutchinson, 2005). In addition, some studies found that consumers appreciate more choice, and favor larger over smaller assortments. These studies concluded that stores offering a large variety of product options are more likely to have greater sales numbers than stores offering less variety (Arnold, Oum, & Tigert, 1983; Brown, Read, & Summers, 2002; Chernev, 2003a; Craig, Gosh, & McLafferty, 1984; Hutchinson, 2005; Kahn, 1995; Koelemeijer & Oppewal, 1999; Mazursky & Jacoby, 1986). Moreover, Kahn and Wansink (2004) demonstrated that when children and adults perceive a store's candy assortment as large, they consume more sweets.

In their meta-analysis, Scheibehenne, Greifeneder, and Todd (2010) could not, on a repeated basis, identify conditions that provide answers to when and why an increase in assortment size will decrease (or increase) the motivation to choose, preference strength, or choice satisfaction. However, this does not mean that choice overload effects do not exist. Instead, existing claims must be examined more parsimoniously, and future research must support these claims with more evidence.

1.5 Managing Overchoice

On the one hand, overchoice can be beneficial in allowing people to have enough alternatives to find what they want or what is good enough for them. On the other hand, overchoice can be overwhelming, confusing, and even unhealthy, and can lead to bad consumer decisions. This negative side of overchoice demands that consumers discover how to manage overchoice and use the abundance of choices to their advantage.

One way to manage this excess of options is to utilize a well-designed choice architecture (Thaler & Sunstein, 2008). People who influence other peoples' decisions are choice architects. Because humans influence choices, human behavior should be incorporated in the construction of choice architecture. It is important to determine who uses this infrastructure, pays for the decision, and profits from the decision (Thaler & Sunstein, 2008). In short, a choice architecture is a structure that is put in place to help people with their decision-making. For instance, when hiring a new person, one might use a heuristic rule (rule of thumb) such as "never judge a book by its cover" or "never judge a job candidate by his/her first impression," to arrive at a decision. A more sophisticated choice architecture might help a person arrive at a practical solution by employing a trial and error approach. For example, suppose it is summertime and a consumer visits a popular ice cream store that offers many different ice cream flavors and combinations. From the outset, the consumer might feel overwhelmed by the many flavors. How should they know which flavors and combinations they like? In this case, the ice cream shop might put a choice architecture in place for the customer: the customer can sample different flavors and then, through trial and error, decide which ice cream to purchase.

Another example of a choice architecture is the Course Match system that was put in place by the University of Pennsylvania's Wharton School (to be discussed in more detail in chapter eight). The system helps MBA students choose their preferred elective classes from a set of approximately 250 electives (a good example of an overchoice situation). In this case, the Course Match system acts as a choice architecture designed by the architect, the Wharton Business School. Students enter their course preferences into the computer and an algorithm generates a schedule. When each student is assigned their preferred set of courses, the market clears. With Course Match, students allocate the greatest number of points (e.g., 100 points) to their preferred course, and then give points to other courses in proportion. This computerized system increases decision efficiency and satisfaction among students by optimizing the course-seat allocation for a large number of classes.

The previous examples in this section raise the following question: how can one prevent or combat the problems that emerge when faced with overchoice? In a magazine article, Iyengar and Agrawal (2010) recommend the following to cope with excess choice:

1. Decrease the number of options to a manageable size.
2. Pay attention to experts or specific recommendations.
3. Categorize options in order to better comprehend the alternatives offered.
4. Learn to work with complex options. (p. 1)

More concerned with the psychology of overchoice, Schwartz (2004) makes the following suggestions for managing overchoice:

1. Decide which choices really matter
2. Think about what you choose
3. Be satisfied with the good enough choice
4. Do not agonize over things when choosing
5. Stick to what you decide
6. Be pleased with what a choice provides
7. Minimize disappointment over bad choices made
8. Expect to compromise
9. Do not hope for too much
10. Compare yourself less to others
11. Seize the opportunities offered (p. 221)

Many overchoice management tools break down a large decision into a series of smaller ones. Such techniques approach the problem of overchoice incrementally and eliminate a few options at each step. Practical applications of this sequential elimination technique can be observed, for instance, in managerial decision-making and patient counseling (Oostendorp, et al., 2011).

After introducing a number of variables that influence overchoice, the following framework provides a critical lens through which overchoice can be examined, understood, and managed. The framework and its different dimensions were mostly conceived from the theoretical scaffolding presented in this chapter, and the psychological, sociological, and economic conceptualizations developed throughout the previous discussion. One dimension of the framework teases out the overchoice variables that influence choice relationships, such as choice control, decision mechanisms, rational decision-making, choice quality, and choice preferences. The other dimension of the framework is concerned with a sequence of steps through which people progress as they make choices. These steps include stresses that alert people about and precede overchoice, reasons that trigger overhoice, as well as possible solutions that can help alleviate or eliminate overchoice. This sequence is an incremental process which we call the three S's, which stands for stresses, sources, and solutions (stresses that are associated with overchoice; sources that cause overchoice; solutions that solve overchoice).

This framework shows, for instance, how one can think about the relationship between choice control and the stresses that alert people about it, the sources that can cause it, and the solutions that can treat it. For example, the framework allows us to consider the influence (control) that one has over different aspects of their belief-system (religion), such as marriage, food, and material possessions. Different religions (solutions) might have different approaches to help their members with these aspects of life in order to prevent unfaithfulness, disease, and greed. We can also apply the framework to examine the extent to which a decision-maker is involved in the choice-making process. There are many stressors (stresses) that precede and determine the levels of choice involvement, such as the social importance of an item and the monetary value assigned to an item. On one end of the spectrum are items (sources), such as toilet paper, candy, or cleaning supplies that require a minimum level of involvement to purchase, whereas on the other end of the spectrum are items that require a high level of involvement, such buying a house, healthcare plan, or new car.

At the center of the overchoice hypothesis is the choice set size, which can be managed and can result in a positive or negative experience for the consumer.

1.6 References

Anderson, C. (2006). *The long tail.* New York, NY: Hachette Book Group.

Arnold, S. J., Oum, T. H., & Tiger, D. J. (1983). Determinant attributes in retail patronage: Seasonal, temporal, regional, and international comparisons. *Journal of Marketing Research, 20*(2), 149–157.

Benartzi, S., & Thaler, R. (2002). How much is investor autonomy worth? *Journal of Finance, 57* (4), 1593–1616.

Blau, P. M. (1964). *Exchange and power in social life.* New York, NY: John Wiley.

Brown, N., Read, D., & Summers, B. (2002). *One of the better-known bits: The lure of choice.* Unpublished manuscript, Leeds University Business School and London School of Economics.

Chernev, A. (2003a). Product assortment and individual decision processes. *Journal of Personality and Social Psychology, 85*(1), 151–162.

Chernev, A. (2003b). When more is less and less is more: The role of ideal point availability and assortment in consumer choice. *Journal of Consumer Research, 30*(2), 170–183.

Chernev, A., Bockenholt, U., & Goodman, J. (2015). Choice overload: A conceptual review and meta-analysis. *Journal of Consumer Psychology, 25*(2), 333–358.

Coleman, S., & O'Sullivan, P. (1990). *William Morris and news from nowhere: A vision of our time.* Cambridge, England: Green Books.

Craig, C. S., Ghosh, A., & McLafferty, S. (1984). Models of the retail location process: A review. *Journal of Retailing, 60*(1), 5–36.

Decety, J., & Casioppo, J. T. (2011). *The Oxford handbook of social neuroscience.* New York, NY: Oxford University Press.

Dennett, D. C. (1997). *Kinds of minds: Toward an understanding of consciousness.* New York, NY: Basic Books.

Dhar, R. (1997). Consumer preference for a no-choice option. *Journal of Consumer Research, 24*(2), 215–231.

Diehl, K. (2005). When two rights make a wrong: Searching too much in ordered environments. *Journal of Marketing Research, 42*(3), 313–322.

Diehl, K., Kornish, L. J., & Lynch Jr., J. G. (2003). Smart agents: When lower search costs for quality information increase price sensitivity. *Journal of Consumer Research, 30*(1), 56–71.

Elster, J. (1989). *The cement of society*. Cambridge, England: Cambridge University Press.

Fromm, E. (1941). *Escape from freedom*. New York, NY: Henry Holt and Company.

Gourville, J. T., & Soman, D. (2005). Overchoice and assortment type: When and why variety backfires. *Marketing Science, 24*(3), 382–395.

Haynes, G. A. (2009). Investigating the dynamics of choice overload. *Psychology and Marketing, 26*(3), 204–212.

Heath, A. (1976). *Rational choice and social exchange*. Cambridge, England: Cambridge University Press.

Homan, S. G. (1971). Attraction and power. In B. I. Murstein (Ed.), *Theories of attraction and love* (pp. 46-52). New York, NY: Springer Publishing.

Hirsch, F. (1976). *Social limits to growth*. Cambridge, MA: Harvard University Press.

Hutchinson, J. (2005). Is more choice always desirable? Evidence and arguments from Leks, Food Selection, and Environmental Enrichment. *Biological Reviews, 80*(1), 73–92.

Iyengar, S. (2010). *The art of choosing*. New York, NY: Twelve, Hachette Book Group.

Iyengar, S., & Agrawal, K. (2010). A better choosing experience. *Strategy+Business Magazine, 61*(Winter), 1–8.

Iyengar, S., Jiang, W., & Huberman, G. (2004). How much choice is too much? Contributions to 401(k) retirement plans. In O. Mitchell & S. Utkus (Eds.), *Pension Design and structure: New lessons from behavioral finance* (pp. 83-96). Oxford, England: Oxford University Press.

Iyengar, S., & Lepper, M. R. (1999). Rethinking the value of choice: A cultural perspective on intrinsic motivation. *Journal of Personality and Social Psychology, 76*(3), 349–366.

Iyengar, S., & Lepper, M. R. (2000). When choice is demotivating: Can one desire too much of a good thing? *Journal of Personality and Social Psychology, 79*(6), 995–1006.

Kahn, B. E. (1995). Consumer variety-seeking among goods and services: An integrative review. *Journal of Retailing and Consumer Services, 2*(3), 139–148.

Kahn, B. E., & Wansink, B. (2004). The influence of assortment structure on perceived variety and consumption quantities. *Journal of Consumer Research, 30*(4), 519–533.

Koelemeijer, K., & Oppewal, H. (1999). Assessing the effects of assortment and ambience: A choice experimental approach. *Journal of Retailing, 75*(3), 319–345.

Lehmann, D. R. (1998). Marketing in the 21st century, commentary; Customer reactions to variety: Too much of a good thing? *Journal of the Academy of Marketing Science, 26*(1), 62–65.

Mazursky, D., & Jacoby, J. (1986). Exploring the development of store images. *Journal of Retailing, 62*(2), 145–165.

5MetaCom (2007). Offering customer too many choices can be a mistake [Newsletter]. *Marketing Insights.* No. 5MC14405.

Miller, G. (1956). The magical number seven, plus or minus two: Some limits on the capacity for processing information. *The Psychological Review, 63*(2), 81–97.

Mischel, W., Ebbesen, E. B., & Raskoff Zeiss, A. (1972). Cognitive and attentional mechanisms in delay of gratification. *Journal of Personality and Social Psychology, 21*(2), 204–218.

The Nielsen Company (2009, June 17). Television Audience 2008. Retrieved from http://www.nielsen.com/content/dam/corporate/us/en/newswire/uploads/2009/07/tva_2008_071709.pdf

Oostendorp, L. J. M., Ottevanger, P. B., van der Graaf, W., & Stalmeier, P. F. M. (2011). The benefits of discussing adjuvant therapies one at a time instead of all at once. *Breast Cancer Research and Treatment, 129*(1), 79–87.

Parson, T. (1937). *The structure of social action.* New York, NY: McGraw-Hill.

Payne, J. (1982). Contingent decision behavior. *Psychological Bulletin, 92*(2), 382–402.

Payne, J. W., Bettman, J. R., & Johnson, E. J. (1988). Adaptive strategy selection in decision making. *Journal of Experimental Psychology: Learning, Memory, and Cognition, 14*(3), 534–552.

Payne, J. W., Bettman, J. R., & Johnson, E. J. (1993). *The adaptive decision maker: Effort and accuracy in choice.* Cambridge, England: Cambridge University Press.

Reutskaja, E. (2008). *Experiments on the role of the number of alternatives in choice* (Unpublished doctoral dissertation). University of Pompeu Fabra, Barcelona, Spain.

Reutskaja, E., & Hogarth, R. M. (2009). Satisfaction in choice as a function of the number of alternatives: When "goods satiate." *Psychology and Marketing, 26*(3), 197–203.

Rose, N. (1999). *Powers of freedom: Reframing political thought.* Cambridge, England: Cambridge University Press.

Satz, D., & Ferejohn, J. (1994). Rational choice and social theory. *The Journal of Philosophy, 91*(2), 71–87.

Scheibehenne, B., Greifeneder, R., & Todd, P. M. (2010). Can there ever be too many options? A meta-analytic review of choice overload. *Journal of Consumer Research,* 3(October), 409–425.

Schwartz, B. (2000). Self-determination: The tyranny of freedom. *American Psychologist, 55*(1), 79–88.

Schwartz, B. (2004). *The paradox of choice: Why more is less.* New York, NY: Harper Collins.

Scott, J. (2000). Rational choice theory. In G. Browning, A. Halcli, & F. Webster (Eds.), *Understanding contemporary society: Theories of the present* (pp. 126-138). London, England: Sage Publications.

Shah, A. M., & Wolford, G. (2007). Buying behavior as a function of parametric variation of number of choices. *Psychological Science, 18*(5), 369–370.

Simon, H. A. (1955). A behavioral model of rational choice. *Quarterly Journal of Economics, 69*(1), 99–118.

Simon, H. A. (1976). *Administrative behavior* (3rd ed.). New York, NY: The Free Press.

Stanovich, K. E. (2009). *What intelligence tests miss: The psychology of rational thought.* Yale, CT: Yale University Press.

Thaler, S. E., & Sunstein, C. (2008). *Nudge: Improving decisions about health, wealth, and happiness.* Yale, CT: Yale University Press.

Timmermans, D. (1993). The impact of task complexity on information use in multi-attribute decision making. *Journal of Behavioral Decision Making,* 6(2), 95–111.

Toffler, A. (1970). *Future shock.* New York, NY: Random House.

Townsend, C., & Kahn, B. E. (2014). The visual preference heuristic: The influence of visual versus verbal depiction on assortment processing, perceived variety, and choice overload. *Journal of Consumer Research, 40*(5), 993–1015.

Weber, M. (1920/1968). Conceptual exposition. In G. Roth & C. Wittich (Eds.), *Economy and society* (pp. 63-309). New York, NY: Bedminister Press. (Original work published 1920)

Wright, P. (1975). Consumer choice strategies: Simplifying vs. optimizing. *Journal of Marketing Research, 12*(1), 60–67.

CHAPTER II

The Story of Desire

Sociological Explorations into Overchoice

Eve Spangler

2.1 The Sociological Roots and Marketing

> Happiness is just the moment before you want more happiness.
>
> — "Commissions and Fees", Don Draper, *Mad Men*, Fifth Season, 2012

Desire is both created and satisfied through social processes. Marketing is the discipline within business schools that addresses the creation and satisfaction of desire. Jerome McCartney (1960) describes the classic tools of marketing as competence in integrating product, price, place, and promotion. Sociology, in turn, focuses on understanding how individual lives both shape and are shaped by society. Therefore, sociology is one of the key intellectual foundations of marketing. The purpose of this chapter is to explore the ways in which the classics of sociological theory provide the rich substrate of ideas that inform activities of effective marketing and the study of marketing (the creation and satisfaction of desire), and to explore overchoice as a socio-cultural and economic phenomenon. The challenge for all of us is to recognize the socially constructed character of desire and to find ways to satisfy it without creating a burdensome world of overchoice, both foisted upon us through manipulation and internalized through our own over-reaching.

Every discipline presents a distinctive view of the human experience, and many of them, having begun with simpler, monocausal models, today employ some version of a complex systems theory. Biologists see humans as a complex physical whole of interrelated subsystems (neurological, muscular-skeletal, digestive, reproductive, etc.) that interact in complex ways, both internally and in response to the outside environment (Alberghina & Westerhoff, 2005; Kaneko, 2006; Rosen, 1968). Psychologists see us as balancing opposing individual drives, while taking into account the demands of those around us (Barker, 1978; Bateson, 1979; DeGreen & Alluisi, 1970). Economists posit a rationally calculating, profit (or satisfaction) maximizing individual, *homo economicus,* who seeks material and social gain in all interactions (Auyang, 1998; Conklin, 1991; Samuelson & Nordhaus, 2004), many of which are characterized by incomplete information and uncertain results. Political scientists explore the ways in which humans seek power and control over their environment, including their neighbors, usually through governmental instruments (Burchill, 2009; Easton, 1965; Kaplan, 1968). Theologians see us as an instrument, part of a complex divine plan for the existence of all beings (Locker, 2011; Tausch & Prager, 1993).

Each of these disciplines, all of them older than sociology, began with a view of humans as maximizing something—power, profit, pleasure, or sanctity. Each discipline, in turn, has had to broaden its focus to acknowledge that human behavior is shaped by the interaction of many forces and hence disciplines require some variant to systems theory to do their explanatory work. Even when humans are driven by a single imperative, people operate with imperfect information and therefore in an environment of indeterminacy and complexity. Each of these disciplines also entertains the hope that its model of interconnection allows for deliberate, strategic, and effective interventions to improve the human condition (Brunner, 1996; Brunner & Barth, 1946; Hein, 2011; Maturano & Varela, 1987; Omenn, 2006; Snooks, 1999).

Sociology emerged later than the disciplines named above, in the context of the great transformation wrought in Europe by the combined forces of industrialism, urbanism, and nationalism. Sociology, therefore, was born in complexity and strove, from the beginning, to be more comprehensive than other disciplines. To some degree, this comprehensiveness is achieved simply by claiming a territory that includes all of human experience: not only the market or the state, not only the psyche or the spirit, but, rather, the sum total of all aspects of human experience in its entirety.

More importantly, however, the sociological aspiration to comprehensiveness rests not simply on staking a claim to a long list of institutions and behaviors, but on the capacity to examine what others take for granted. Sociologists agree with economists that yes, people do act often to maximize material or social gains. But our understanding of human behavior is incomplete until we have also accounted for the very creation of desire: how is it that some goods or services or social positions come to be valued, while others are not. (The relevance of this insight for marketing is immediately apparent.) Sociologists agree with political scientists and psychologists that yes, human beings often do seek control over their physical and social environment. But our understanding is incomplete until we can account for the processes whereby some groups of people come to equate control with military power, while others seek control through spiritual harmony with their environment. Sociology thus seeks to address not only substantive knowledge, but also the processes by which knowledge of all sorts—expert and lay—is created. Because of this preoccupation with the social construction of reality, (Berger & Luckmann, 1966) sociology is the wellspring of marketing expertise.

The sociological story begins with the recognition that humans, despite their biological separateness, are profoundly social beings. Children are born in a state of extreme dependency; they cannot secure their existence on their own, but must rely on their relationships with parents or other caregivers in order to survive. Human life, therefore, is necessarily social from the moment of birth. Even such seemingly physical milestones of infant development as the control of head motion, the ability to turn over, or to make limbs move intentionally, have a large social component and depend on encouragement and reinforcement from caregivers. Moreover, simple motor control is only a tiny part of human development. All of the more complex actions we learn to perform—to speak our native language, ride a bicycle, make friends, work on a computer, court a mate, resolve differences, hold a job, participate in the civic life around us, grow old gracefully—require even more interaction with others.

The giants of early American sociology, George Herbert Mead and Charles Horton Cooley, provide us with the concepts that describe the development of a social self. Together, their work offers us the notions of a "looking glass self" (Cooley, 1902) formed out of interactions with significant and generalized others (Mead, 1956).

It is to the infant's advantage to understand quickly what caregivers like or dislike, to internalize those preferences, and to act accordingly. Compliant behavior causes caregivers to express approval and to exert themselves further on the infant's behalf. Through these interactions, the infant comes to develop a sense of self that is shaped only in small part by his or her own bodily feelings, and, more importantly, by the behavior of others. In short, we develop a "looking glass self" based on what other people mirror back to us about our identity. Are we good boys or girls or do we hear a lot of "no, no, no?" Do caregivers respond to us at all or ignore our needs? Are we praised for beauty, intelligence, or strength? The answers to such questions allow other people to tell us who we are. Even lay people recognize the seductive quality of looking in the mirror to discover themselves and to name their deepest needs—mirrors figure in mythology all the way from Snow White (Grimm brothers) to Harry Potter's Mirror of Erised ("desire," spelled backwards) (Rowling, 1998).

At first, the circle of people who shape our self-perception is small and intimate, consisting mostly of family and friends. These people are the most significant group to reflect back information about ourselves, both because they appear on the scene before all others, and because we have sustained, life-long interactions with them. George Herbert Mead refers to these early and most important partners as "significant others." But gradually we all move from the small circle of home into a larger world of teachers, classmates, neighbors, employers, store clerks, fellow bus or train passengers, friends of friends on Facebook, etc. They, too, have expectations of us and mirror back to us a sense of who we are and whether our behavior is pleasing to them. This larger circle of people who populate our lives are the "generalized other" in Mead's terminology.

Given media penetration of our lives, the generalized other can even include people whom we never meet and know only at second hand. The opinions and preferences of a global "generalized other" provide a running commentary on our existence and impinge on our sense of identity.

Consider, for example, the ways in which government figures at home and abroad shape our identities. Are we liberty-loving Americans, as George Bush told us when he asserted that "they" hate us for our freedom? Or was the late Hugo

Chavez closer to the truth in telling us that we are ugly Americans, hateful neo-colonial exploiters? Our sense of national identity is constructed not only from the simple geographic fact of residence, or even the bureaucratic fact of which state issues our passport, but through the conversation with a global generalized other known via the media.

Similarly, our private social and economic identities are constructed, in part, through media-defined narratives. Magazines perused at the dentist's office show us what our homes should look like. Billboards suggest the kind of accoutrements we need to signal to others that we are hip and cool, or conservative and traditional. Television shows carry messages about how we should organize leisure and worship.

To summarize: followers of Cooley and Mead argue that our sense of our own identity is neither fixed nor immanent, unfolding from within. Instead, it is rooted in and arises out of our social interactions with others. First, we imagine how we appear to others (both intimate and distant). Second, we imagine the judgments of those others about what they see. Third, we develop a sense of ourselves based on those judgments. Whether we are determined to live up to them or to thwart them, we are never indifferent to the opinion of others (Yeung & Martin, 2003), and we are never deaf to the messages those opinions and responses contain about our own identities.

The insights of Cooley and Mead were systematized and expanded by theorists who created the "symbolic interactionist" school of sociology (Becker, 1970; Blumer, 1969). The central insight of symbolic interaction is this: just as with the self, the meaning of objects and relationships is constructed through social interaction. Parallel to the three precepts of Cooley and Mead, the symbolic interactionists also describe a three-step system of social interaction as follows: 1) humans act toward things on the basis of the meanings they ascribe to those things; 2) the meanings of such things are not inherent, but derive from and arise out of social interaction; and 3) the meanings are forged through an iterative process used by the parties over time (Blumer, 1969, pp. 2-21).

An example of the second and third points is found in the changing use of American flag symbols and men sporting long hair. In the 1960s, a young man sporting a flag symbol— preferably on the seat of his jeans—and wearing his hair long, was signaling membership in a somewhat dissident counterculture. Often that young man risked assault for his symbolic self-presentation. Today, the very men who might have assaulted a "filthy hippie" in the past are themselves sporting flag decals and pony tails, connoting working class and patriotic identities.

Through the work of Cooley, Mead, Blumer, and Becker, sociological theory provides us with a very particular worldview: one in which interaction is not primarily about discovering the inherent meaning of the objects and relationships around us. Rather, interaction is a process of negotiating identity and meaning, of co-creating our world through our relations with others, past, present, and imagined. We not only have looking glass selves, we live in a looking glass world. In this world, reality has an emergent property: it is not reducible to behavior dictated by the biological or psychological characteristics of individuals, but arises out of the flow of everyday interaction in its infinite variability.

Clearly, a looking glass world is one in which marketing can flourish. It is one in which need is not fixed by biological nature; on the contrary, desire (and products) are defined socially. It is a world in which value (and price) is subject to negotiation and renegotiation. It is a world in which context (place) includes an infinite variety of lifestyles, identities and commodities. It is a world in which media saturation (promotion) allows every person to live with a vast reference group encompassing all human communities; one richly populated by objects and technologies from many cultures whose role in our lives remains to be negotiated.

The pliability of the world, as described by the theorists above, presents both opportunities and challenges for individuals. If the meaning of objects and relations arises through negotiated interactions, then every individual has some power in naming their reality. But this freedom is also burdensome. It requires us to choose continually where and how to allocate our attention; where and how to engage in the struggle to change our understanding of objects and events around us, or to let conventional definitions, perhaps forged by others, stand. Do we train ourselves to attend, in real time, to interactions that make us uncomfortable? Do we challenge racist or homophobic or Islamophobic language around us? Do we comment on the gendered uses of violence in blockbuster movies? Do we share skepticism about political or advertising rhetoric?

The German sociologist and phenomenologist Arnold Gehlen has devoted his work to thinking through the consequences of the socially constructed nature of our world (Berger & Kellner, 1965; Gehlen, 1988). He begins from the premise that our capacity to pay attention is finite and the possible world of meaning infinite. Gehlen coined the term "sensory overload" to describe the dilemmas created by this juxtaposition. "Overchoice" might be considered a synonym. He concludes that we need systematic, reliable routines and habits for allocating attention; for deciding what we will think about critically and intentionally and where and when we will let habit reign. He argues that we divide up the world into a taken-for-granted background where we act without much reflection, and a foreground where we are aware of making choices.

Let us follow someone through the day: We become aware of being awake and do not make labored decisions about whether to put our right or left foot down first when we arise. We probably do not think about whether we will shower, brush teeth, or eat breakfast first. We may not even make much conscious choice in preparing breakfast. Likely we pay more attention to dressing and perhaps we do not pay enough attention to take along the book we meant to return to the library on our lunch hour. We drive to work, probably at some moments not aware consciously of the route we have chosen. We arrive at work and do not notice the color of our office walls, or the choice of technology on our desk—we simply get to work, choosing to attend to the content of emails or voicemails, but not to the decision whether to do this early in the work day or later. We take habitual seats at departmental meetings and in the cafeteria. We have to enter dates in our diaries or phone calendars to keep our commitments straight. In the evening our routines continue to unspool. Every one of these implicit decisions about what to ignore and where to pay attention could be rethought—but then life would become impossibly burdensome. Building on Cooley and Mead, Becker, and Blumer, Gehlen's work provides us an anthropological—perhaps even a neurological—basis for thinking about the balance between choice and overchoice, the point at which we can have too much of a good thing.

But, positing a tipping point between a desirable level of choice and a burdened sense of overchoice is not simply an individual anthropological or neurological problem. Yes, the world gets constructed through the infinitely varied interpretive acts of its participants, but, equally, it gets constructed within a context in which some individuals have vastly more power than others, whether in "defining reality" or in acquiring material resources, or in controlling the machinery of government.

2.2 Marx

Karl Marx is perhaps the single most important theorist to insist that the reality-creating activities of human beings have to be understood in the context of inequalities of wealth and power. "Men make their own history," he says (in the 18th Brumaire of Louis Bonaparte) "but they do not make it just as they please; they do not make it under circumstances chosen by themselves, but under circumstances found, given, and transmitted from the past" (as cited in Tucker, 1978, p. 595).

Class differentiation is the most significant condition that is given and transmitted from the past. In Marx's world (in the Manifesto of the Communist Party), society is "more and more splitting up into two great hostile camps, into two great classes directly facing each other: Bourgeoisie and Proletariat" (as cited in Tucker, 1978, p. 474).

Such a statement will seem, at first glance, to be a vast oversimplification. Even the most orthodox Marxists have come to recognize the need for more subtlety, and therefore posit that the "two great contending classes" are further subdivided into class fractions. Marx himself drew distinctions in the 18th Brumaire, cited above, between the aristocracies of land and capital—between the workers or proletariat and the chronically unemployed or lumpenproletariat—and he left room for other groups who occupied distinctive roles in the system of production, such as soldiers and clergy.

The value of Marxist thinking lies less in specific depictions of the class structure, and more in the way he expanded classical theories of capitalism, which viewed the market as a realm of freedom and creativity. While not denying the freedom and especially the creativity, Marx also saw markets as realms of exploitation, injustice and, with them, conflict and contradiction. His theory, including extensions by later-day Marxists, continues to furnish an insightful roadmap to the workings of global capitalism.

Marx begins with a materialist premise. He posits that people exist as physical beings that must, first of all, secure their material livelihood. A society that does not provide at least minimal food, clothing, and shelter to its members cannot long survive. Put simply, we must eat in order to live, and we must work in order to eat. In Marx's words (in the German Ideology), "Men can be distinguished from animals by consciousness, by religion or anything else you like. They themselves begin to distinguish themselves from animals as soon as they begin to produce their means of subsistence" (as cited in Tucker, 1978, p. 150).

Because of our material nature and the needs it imposes on our existence, work is, for Marx, the central category of human experience. Work is our fate and destiny; its organization defines the quality of our community.

To his materialist premise, Marx adds a historical perspective. Over time, the basic ways in which we have organized ourselves to produce our material world have evolved from technologically unsophisticated hunting and gathering tribes (called "primitive communists" in Marxist theory), to agricultural, and then to industrial societies.

This history, however, is not one of simple progress. True, technology has become ever more sophisticated and has produced enormous wealth. In Marx's words (in the Manifesto of the Communist Party), capitalism "has accomplished wonders far surpassing Egyptian pyramids, Roman aqueducts, and Gothic cathedrals; ... [it] has created more massive and more colossal productive forces than have all preceding generations together" (as cited in Tucker, 1978, pp. 476-477).

At the same time that wealth has grown, however, social injustice has grown along with it. Great wealth exists in tandem with great poverty, even when productivity is such that no one need be denied. Marx refers to this phenomenon as "immiserization." The city of Boston, where this chapter is being written, provides a poignant example. Home to some of the most prestigious teaching hospitals in the world, much of the infant mortality in this city occurs almost literally within the shadow of elite health care organizations. How is it that so many babies are left to die in a city that hosts foreign royalty when they need surgery? If humans construct their own society, why do they produce such a tragic juxtaposition of poverty and plenty? Why would anyone acquiesce to such an unjust arrangement?

Marx provides a powerful way of understanding this paradox. He argues that once humanity moved out of its early, quasi-endemic phase of hunting and gathering, the means of production came to be privately owned. Whether this occurred through raiding and warfare as some Marxists argue (Diamond, 1971), or by some other means lost in pre-history, the fact remains that all agricultural and industrial societies are marked by a class division between the owners of the society's productive instruments and those excluded from such ownership. Thus, a small group monopolizes control over the tools needed to be economically productive, thereby reducing the rest of society to people who command only their own labor power and who must come to terms with the owning class in order to secure a job. This development—private ownership not of consumer goods or trinkets, but of the instruments for securing a livelihood—reduces most people to the role of supplicants and constitutes the original sin of the Marxist universe.

Once an economy is divided between owners and workers, conflict ensues. The owners must secure profits in order to survive. This imperative is non-negotiable and exists irrespective of their personal temperament. They may be brilliant or dull, generous or stingy, humorous or grim, humane or callous, but they must earn a profit to succeed as owners. This imperative gives them a stake in holding down the cost of production, especially wages. On the other side of the class divide, the worker, also without personal villainy, needs the highest possible wages for his or her own family. Enter class warfare at the point of production, i.e. in the workplace (Wooding & Levenstein, 1999). The economist Richard Edwards summarizes this argument very simply: the workplace becomes a contested terrain (Edwards, 1979).

The struggle for control in the workplace can take many forms. On the part of owners, strategies can include direct oversight, or a choice of tools that compel workers to produce at a certain pace (think of Charlie Chaplin's little tramp on the assembly line) or in a specified fashion (any pre-programmable tool). Owners can also manipulate bureaucratic rules and rewards in order to insure compliance (Edwards, 1979). The struggle for control may take other social forms as well, leading to the redesign of jobs in the direction of de-skilling (Braverman, 1974) or the promoting of social conflict among workers of different genders or races (e.g. Spangler, 1992). On the part of workers, strategies can include collective action such as unionization, individual resistance and even sabotage or pilfering, gaming the system (e.g. Burawoy, 1979; Chinoy, 1955), working to rule, or leaving the job if necessary.

Despite these conflicts, robust economies emerge during the more successful phases of the business cycle. The world is not always a war of each against all. Individuals, both among workers and owners, make their peace with particular trade-offs, and marketing may play a significant role in defining which tradeoffs are acceptable. Some workers will tolerate less pay for more meaningful work (most educators fall in this category), some will bet on the rewards of extensive higher education, still others will try to exit the system and establish their own small businesses. Among owners, similarly, a variety of accommodations can exist, from the more attractive management styles based on incentives (e.g., employee stock options, generous bonuses, a good benefits package) to the more aversive ones based on coercion.

Temporary solutions to this eternal conflict notwithstanding, the contentious nature of the workplace is further exacerbated by contradictions. Owners not only want low wages in order to minimize their costs of production, they also depend upon affluent consumers in order to realize the profits of their productive efforts. It is no wonder, under these circumstances, that capitalists fear powerful and capricious consumers and want to manage desire with marketing tools. Similarly, workers want high wages but nevertheless seek out low-cost consumer goods, even while knowing that cheap goods imply low wages for other workers. Again, as with the major conflicts, individual accommodations can and do exist within these contradictions. Nevertheless, across the economy as a whole, low wages do not produce affluent consumers, and the market for low-cost consumer goods undercuts the ability to generate high wages.

Taken together, the conflicts and contradictions of the capitalist system ensure that the economy exists in a state of turmoil, a kind of permanent whitewater. Given the inherent instability of the economy, it is easy to predict that work conflicts—"politics at the point of production" (Wooding & Levenstein, 1999) will spill out of the workplace into other sectors of society. Marx predicted this with great clarity, dismissing the government as the executive committee of the bourgeoisie (The Manifesto of the Communist Party) (as cited in Tucker, 1978, p. 475), denouncing education for promoting the ideas of the ruling class (The German Ideology) (as cited in Tucker, 1978, p. 172), and, most famously, criticizing religion as "the opiate of the people" (Introduction to the Critique of Hegel's *Philosophy of Right*) (as cited in Tucker, 1978, p. 54). In this view, many religious, political and cultural conflicts are really only class conflicts playing out in disguised and deflected forms.

If neither the conflicts nor the contradictions of capitalism can be definitively resolved, then the following question arises: why do most people soldier on rather than opting to change the system dramatically? Here too, Marx provides the germ of an answer. In the extreme case, in the face of organized insurrection designed explicitly to overturn the capitalist system, repression can and will be used to eliminate challenges. But recourse to manipulation is far more common. Things will stay the same to the degree that people can be persuaded to believe that things are better than they actually are, or that, in any event, they cannot be changed. Things will stay the same to the degree that people feel that all they really need to be happy is a bigger house, a fancier car, a more exotic vacation. Things will stay the same to the degree that people express a sense of rebelliousness by shopping for tattoos, all-black clothing, or the "goth" look.

Marketing, in all its aspects, may lend itself to being a tool of manipulation. At its worst, it may create products that do little to meet real human needs for dignity or equality; it may encourage self-definitions based on consumption rather than efficacy; it can develop price systems that engender eternal indebtedness and, correlatively, political quiescence; it may encourage attitudes that view the earth as an inexhaustible warehouse rather than a fragile planet.

On the other hand, marketing could—and sometimes does—marshal its tools for socially responsible purposes. From public service announcements, to branding environmentally sustainable goods, to encouraging consumer skepticism and vigilance, the techniques and skills of marketing can be used to change the world for the better. Whether they will be used in this fashion depends in large measure on the degree to which other forces—grassroots social movements, subversive professionals and civil servants, progressive political parties—demand such action or, at the very least, open a social space for it.

Put differently from a Marxist point of view, the question of "overchoice" is not about the number of choices people have to make in order to get on with their lives. Rather, "overchoice" occurs when people are manipulated into investing a lot of energy in choices, none of which actually enhance their control over their life—when choice is severed from power and efficacy. In the business world, this phenomenon is sometimes described as "marginal product differentiation." I can spend a lot of time comparing color, trim, or entertainment systems in the car I wish to purchase. What I cannot get, no matter how astute and attentive a consumer I am, is the choice between private and public systems of transportation, or between democratic and integrative road design or highways that also isolate minority communities and neglect their infrastructure.

Marx, in short, raises the question about the relationship between the appearance of individual or group choice and the real exercise of power in our communities. The existence of a conflicted global form of capitalism is, for the moment, a given, whereas the presence of effective movements for social justice is more problematic. This context, so clearly depicted by Marx, creates a powerful undertow for marketing, pulling it toward the manufacturers' need to control the creation and satisfaction of desire in the face of economic and political uncertainty—in short, to routinely create situations of "overchoice."

2.3 Weber

Moreover, even if marketing were to commit to a social justice agenda, the work of the great German sociologist Max Weber sounds a cautionary note. Karl Marx saw capitalism as deeply flawed, yet he also thought that his analysis of what went wrong pointed the way to setting things right. If the original sin is the separation of ownership of the means of production from labor, then the solution is to reunite them in the form of collective, communal ownership of the means of production.

Weber, writing a generation after Marx, is far less sanguine and certainly holds out no hope that socialism would produce a better world than capitalism has done. Indeed, his conclusion about any future grounded in industrialism (in Politics as a Vocation) is this: "Not summer's bloom lies ahead, but a polar night of icy darkness and hardness" (as cited in Gerth & Mills, 1958, p. 128).

Weber essentially takes Marx's analysis as a point of departure. The economy is indeed divided between owners and workers (and their respective subgroups), and it does produce a paradoxical system of poverty in the face of plenty. But, according to Weber, it does so in an even more subtly disastrous way than Marx predicts. Not only is there a conflict between owners and workers but also a contradiction between stingy employers who need affluent consumers and ambitious workers who eek out cheap consumer goods that rely on low wage work. In addition to these structural considerations, there is also a culture—embraced by owners and workers alike—that exists within the realm of industrialism and that brings little good to anyone despite the dazzling increase in productivity associated with the industrial age.

In Weber's (1958) vast, sweeping review of world history, he alights on the Protestant Reformation as the beginning of our troubled times. Viewed in hindsight, the Reformation, of course, broke the unity of the Catholic Church into competing Christian denominations, with enormous consequences for the relationships between church and state. But, prospectively, the Reformation was about reforming the corruption of the Catholic Church of the sixteenth century. While various lay people and clergy challenged the visible forms of corruption (for example, the sale of indulgences), two key theologians—Martin Luther and Jean Calvin—took it upon themselves to close the theological loopholes from which the corruption sprang.

Specifically, they were concerned that recourse to "faith" was not enough to reconcile the apparent contradiction between the church's teaching about moral choice—namely that we are all to act as though we have free will and can be held accountable for the behaviors we chose—and its equally insistent positing of an omniscient deity. Obviously, if a deity is truly omniscient, then foreknowledge of our seemingly freely chosen behavior would constitute a part, albeit a minute part, of the "all" that the deity foreknows.

The early Protestant theologians cut this Gordian knot by insisting on predestination. The omniscience of the deity means that our behavior is, in fact, predestined even when we, in our ignorance, experience it as freely chosen. (As a practical matter, the insistence on predestination also cut the intellectual ground out from under the sale of indulgences. If we are predestined, then neither good works nor corrupt ones, like bribery, will buy our way into heaven).

Immediately, a theology of predestination creates an enormous pragmatic problem. If my behavior is indeed predestined, might I not be predestined to sleep late today, to stay away from work, to act in an entirely self-serving and anti-social way? In order to obviate this threat to an orderly world, the Protestant theologians posited a doctrine of vocation—or calling—along with an insistence on predestination.

The idea of vocation posited that human beings were part of the deity's plan for creation—instruments of the divine will. Our job in life was to discover the germ of talent within ourselves—which is a gift from God—and to use that talent to do God's work in the world. Note that this formulation requires not only a continuous, unceasing hard work, but also permits, indeed *requires*, innovative work; our talents, literally God's gifts, must not be squandered on mere routine.

The purpose of earthly striving is not financial reward, and certainly not the enjoyment of consumer goods. Instead, even for ordinary people, the purpose of earthly striving is to demonstrate our alignment with God's plan for the world, thereby signaling to others—and, perhaps more importantly, to ourselves—that we are predestined for salvation rather than damnation. Remember, because we have a looking glass self, convincing ourselves and convincing others are inevitably intertwined processes. The Protestant universe, Weber (1958) argued, is a place where we work not for paltry material rewards, but as if our very souls depended upon it.

In the sense that Weber posited a Protestant ethic that sanctifies work, almost everyone in America is culturally Protestant, whether they worship in a church, or a synagogue, or a mosque, or an ashram, or not at all. Nearly all of us believe in the moral superiority of work over idleness. This is demonstrated in our everyday culture in many ways: in bragging about how "crazy busy" we are, that we never take a sick day off at work, that we do not use all our vacation days, that our leisure activities are justified primarily to the degree that they prevent burnout, i.e. the capacity for more work. (Innovation is, perhaps, more suspect than hard work, in part because it is so hard to know prospectively which innovations will prove to be fruitful, but also because innovation has the potential to unsettle routines and challenge privilege. We all want newer and better ways of doing things, but only as long as our social standing and power are not diminished).

Given the Protestant ethic in either its religious or secular form, people became willing to work in ways that they never have before. Work is now a continuous, unending obligation in its own right, and is decoupled from material need. Whereas hunter-gatherers worked when need and opportunity converged, they also created leisure intensive communities outside of the hunting season. Work was intermittent and related to basic needs in obvious ways. This is completely unlike modern societies in which most people work continuously, way past the point where their material needs are satisfied. Who among us has not stood in front of a closet full of clothes and said, "I have nothing to wear." How many of us own sports equipment we are too busy to use?

But again, the question arises: if human beings construct the social world, why don't they get off the treadmill? Why don't they see through the manipulations and the creation of fake needs? Why don't they, following Peter Finch's character in the film *Network*, throw open the window and cry, "I've had enough, and I'm not going to take it anymore."

Here Weber offers two other dimensions that anchor our culture of perpetual toil. First, he argues that the early Protestant theologians broadcast their ideas at a very particular moment in history. Their exhortations were taken up by common people who lived in an explosively expanding economy. This context is crucial because in a growing economy, hard work, especially when it is innovative, often *is* rewarded by economic success. And success, in turn, seems to validate Protestant teachings. Despite the fact that Protestant theologians decried the idea that God gave signs of salvation or damnation, and were certainly appalled by the notion that wealth was a sign of God's favor, the Protestant laity chose to come to its own conclusions. If eternal toil is sanctified, they reasoned, why should the rewards of that toil not also participate in the sacred? Wealth came to be seen as a sign of election and thereby the notion that you must work as if your soul depended upon it grew in strength and credibility.

The time and place are also significant because the economy was growing in a very particular way—transitioning from a predominantly agricultural society with small towns and a trickle of trade in luxuries, to a predominantly industrial economy based on factory production and market exchange. Industry differs from agriculture and hunting/gathering in many crucial ways. The one that concerns us here is the issue of control.

In general it is true that industrious, attentive hunters do better than sloppy ones, and hard-working farmers—who water and weed, burn smudge pots against the cold, and construct arbors over their plants against the scorching sun—do better than those who laze their way through the day. Yet no hunter or farmer would ever argue that they are in total control of their productivity. Hunters know that animals shift their migratory routes, or develop new diseases, or starve for lack of forage. Farmers know that, despite their best efforts, droughts, floods, fires, locusts will take their share of the crop.

Only in industrial society can humans believe credibly that they alone control production in its entirety—choosing ingredients, proportions, and manufacturing processes that guarantee the outcome. The experience of total control in one significant area of life (production) is utterly seductive and, according to Weber, leads human communities to overextend the notion of control to encompass not only production, but also distribution and, indeed, all phases of life.

Weber thus shows us how three strands entwine to make up the fabric of industrial society. Work comes to be understood as a sacred rather than a merely practical activity, thereby unleashing a ferocious work ethic that accepts no limits to the amount of effort that we expect of ourselves. The result of losing such a work ethic into a world of expanding economic opportunity is to sanctify not only vast fortunes but innovative production techniques as well. And the combination of wealth and innovation, in turn, produces a full blown industrial system that appears to reward an ethos of total control and planning, at least over one of life's most important domains—the world of work.

Once we are in thrall to the quest for complete control over all aspects of life, overchoice becomes inevitable. We lose all capacity to be at peace with aspects of life we do not control, and strain to control that which is not controllable. We no longer have the choice to be fatalistic (or we risk being labeled as deviant if we so choose), but must exert control in all things. We see examples of this all around us: pregnant couples who play French tapes to their unborn child in order to create more facility with language learning, and who drill infants with flash cards for early reading. Coaching becomes a major form of consulting for leisure activities and hobbies, for academic test-taking, or for job interviews. People are exhorted to dress for success, but never to join unions, or to ask why there are not enough good jobs for everyone willing to work.

For those who celebrate capitalism (e.g., Gilder, 1993), this explosion of work, wealth, and control is a consummation they really envisioned. Weber disagrees. He argues that, by a series of unintended consequences, the very success of industrialism has created a society dominated by technical rationality at the expense of value rationality. All of the institutions that serve technical rationality—e.g., science, higher education, contract law, patent and intellectual property rights—have come to be highly developed, while those that would serve value rationality—e.g., religion, the arts—have been permitted to atrophy, leaving us in a world in which we have lost our way. We can travel further and faster, without knowing where we ought to be going. We can produce more and more goods, without distributing them equitably or understanding environmental limits to growth. We can pursue ever more detailed scientific knowledge without taking responsibility for the uses to which our findings are put. This is a world that, for Weber, is disenchanted. He is worth quoting at some length on this point:

> Does it mean that we, today . . . have a greater knowledge of the conditions of life under which we exist than has an American Indian or a Hottentot? Hardly. Unless he is a physicist, one who rides on the streetcar has no idea how the car happened to get into motion... The savage knows incomparably more about his tools . . . . The increasing intellectualization and rationalization do *not*, therefore, indicate an

> increased and general knowledge of the conditions under which one lives...
>
> It means something else, namely, the ... belief that if one but wished one *could* learn it at any time. Hence, it means that principally there are no mysterious incalculable forces that come into play, but rather that one can, in principle, master all things by calculation. This means that the world is disenchanted... One need no longer have recourse to magical means in order to master or implore the spirits ... technical means and calculations perform the service. This above all is what intellectualization means. ("Science as a Vocation," as cited in Gerth & Mills, 1958, p. 138).

For Weber, the world of science is, in the end, arid and amoral, however thrilling its discoveries and productive its application to industry may also be. Science does not, indeed *cannot,* answer what he calls "the only meaningful questions"—"Who should we be and how should we live?"—because the answers to such questions fall outside of the realm of technical calculation. Moreover, science, with its insistence on the unknown but its denigration of the "unknowable," serves to undermine the very discourses—theology, art—that have traditionally provided answers to the only meaningful questions. Thus, in Weber's world, science undermines religion without adequately replacing it. Overchoice arises from this disjunction; the belief that all can be controlled implies a responsibility to choose and to control. And since, in Weber's view, the premise is fundamentally wrong, overchoice is a cursed condition.

Note how, throughout Weber's work, the notion of unintended consequences leads to a pervasive sense of dread. The early Protestant theologians meant to strip the church of its corruption in order to make the hand of God more visible and, through the reinterpretations of their parishioners, their doctrine came to be understood as a sanctification of worldliness. Science seeks to make the world more rational, but instead it removes the question of values from the public discourse, making the world only more technocratic. In the end, Weber (in Science as a Vocation) concludes, "Specialists without spirit, sensualists without heart; this nullity imagines that it has attained a level of civilization never before achieved" (as cited in Gerth & Mills, 1958, p. 182).

Here, Weber's estimation of the quality of modern society comes very close to the tone of Marx's analysis, where he (in The Manifesto of the Communist Party) writes, "The bourgeoisie, wherever it has got the upper hand, has . . . left remaining no other nexus between man and man than naked self-interest, than callous 'cash payment.' It has drowned the most heavenly ecstasies of religious fervor . . . in the icy water of egotistical calculation. It has resolved personal worth into exchange value, and in place of the numberless indefeasible chartered freedoms has set up that single, unconscionable freedom – Free Trade." (as cited in Tucker, 1978, p. 475).

Cumulatively, then, we have a story that shows how human beings construct a sense of self by interacting with others—all within a context of structural inequality and cultural misunderstanding and self-deception. Marx emphasizes the structural sources of injustice: the class conflicts and contradictions that create an oppressive, manipulative, and alienating economy and society. Weber emphasizes the cultural dimensions associated with the institutional arrangements of capitalism. He is vastly more pessimistic than Marx, because he notes how even those oppressed and mistreated by capitalism share its world views and, moreover, because he predicts that socialism—for him just another form of industrialism with the same deadly hubris at its heart—will not be a solution to the dilemmas of capitalism. Marx and Weber differ only in the degree of their pessimism. Marx, believing that overchoice is a result of manipulation that could be corrected, is relatively less grim than Weber, who believes that both the capitalist and socialist versions of industrialism rest on an unrealistic agenda of overcontrol/overchoice that exhausts without enlightening.

2.4 Durkheim

Émile Durkheim, the last of the sociological giants of the early years, adds a further dimension to the study of society. If Marx focused on the dynamics of capitalism and Weber on the dynamics of industrialism, then Durkheim returned to sociology's most ambitious mandate: he is concerned with the question of how any social order is possible.

Like Marx and Weber, Durkheim understands work to be the foundation of society. Also like Mark and Weber, Durkheim is at once charmed by the productivity of our economy, but deeply concerned with its possibly fatal flaws. Durkheim can best be read as accepting the work of Marx—namely that class divisions cause conflict and oppression—and the work of Weber— namely that we buy into an ethos of rational calculation that is inadequate for conversations about justice and is thus, ultimately, irrational. But Durkheim has his own reasons for noting that the problems of contemporary society will resist easy solutions.

Durkheim (1893/1948) focuses on the fact that in modern, high-tech societies, workers are divided not only from owners but also from each other. Our degree of occupational specialization is vast and, to the degree that we are what we do, we and our neighbors, who are differently occupied, have very little common ground. Work divides not only owners from employees, but also professionals from laborers, and managers from both the people they supervise and the people to whom they report. Erik Olin Wright (1985) refers to this as a "contradictory class location," (pp. 37-42). Night shift workers have a distinctive set of lifestyles and even diseases (National Institute of Occupational Safety and Health, 1997). People in the arts think differently from those in the sciences; people in manufacturing have different perspectives from those in service occupations; even within a narrow range of occupations—such as that of craft workers, electricians, carpenters, and plumbers—people have their own distinctive points of view, their own occupational cultures.

On the positive side, Durkheim acknowledges that this specialization allows for greatly enhanced productivity. Specialization also has social and ethical rewards, or so hope would have it. Specialization creates a society in which no one can stand alone. We do not single-handedly grow our own food, build our own houses, and sew our own clothes. We depend on myriad others to do their jobs so that we may live. And because we depend on these many other people, we have a stake in respecting them, and seeing that they are content with their lives—in short, living peacefully and amicably with them. President Barak Obama, in his first presidential campaign, was speaking more to racial than occupational differences, but he captured the spirit of this argument in his slogan, "From the many, we are one." The question, however, is how do we become one from many? How do we live in harmony with people, some of whose existence we do not even know about?

An anecdote will illustrate the point. Some years ago, the teaching assistants at a major state university tired of their meager pay and decided to form a union. The unionization drive occurred at a moment when the Teamsters Union—long associated with gangsterism—was seeking to clean up its image. The Teamsters approached the doctoral students and invited them to affiliate with the Teamsters

Union. Such an affiliation would obligate Teamster drivers to honor graduate student picket lines and stop all deliveries to campus. The deal was struck, the graduate students became Teamsters, and, on the appointed day, the first two trucks to encounter the graduate student picketers turned back instead of continuing on to the campus. By noon, the university folded and recognized the graduate student union.

People not familiar with campus life might wonder what was on those two trucks. Most people will guess at one of them. Typically, they imagine a food truck turning back. In fact, they are partially right. The first truck's load was related to nutrition and digestion; it carried toilet paper.

But no one ever guesses what the second truck carried, because the workings of a major university are so complex and varied that most of us, even university graduates, know very little about what goes in and comes out. To understand the second truck, one needs to understand that universities have three major sources of revenue: tuition, alumni donations, and research overhead (the percentage of research money that goes to maintaining the general capabilities of the university rather than to individual researchers). No university can afford to endanger its research labs and hope to continue securing grants that carry overhead. And so when a truck containing liquid nitrogen—essential for temperature and humidity control in the labs—turned back, the university agreed to recognize the graduate student union.

This story is double-edged. It does, indeed, reveal that people in many different occupations are interdependent in a university, as they are in society. But this story also reveals how easy it is, when occupational specialization becomes elaborate, to miss entirely, misunderstand, or underestimate the complex ways we are interconnected. The connections between graduate students and truckers, and between truckers and researchers, caught the university by surprise.

Durkheim thus worried about the ways in which occupational differentiation eroded the essential common ground for both individuals and societies as a whole. Absent common ground, even people who wish to act well toward their neighbors may not have enough information to do so.

On the individual level, Durkheim worried about anomie—a sense of normlessness that paralyzes us when we are confronted with too much choice. My students often cite the menu of a popular restaurant chain—a veritable catalogue some twenty pages long—as typifying the not-always-delicious pressure of too much choice. What happens when we have to make choices more consequential than the flavor of our dessert in a restaurant? Hardly any aspect of life is devoid of choice. We can change jobs, convert to a different religion, move our residence, surgically alter our personal appearance, reconsider political affiliations, divorce spouses, and start over with new partners. It is now possible, with sex reassignment surgery, even to renegotiate our gender. Can the renegotiation of race be far behind?

Faced with a bewildering array of choices, a complex context in which often we cannot foresee the consequences of our choices, and, finally, the need to choose even the values that will guide our further choices, it is no wonder that a book entitled *Escape From Freedom* (Fromm, 1969) became a best seller. Durkheim (1897/1951), in fact, argues that in extreme cases, this context of too much choice and too little common ground with ones neighbors leads to anomic suicide. Clearly, for him overchoice is the baseline human condition on modern, urban societies and it is a very uncomfortable one, even in the face of material plenty.

Durkheim's argument about anomic suicide is this: All human beings will likely be confronted, over the course of a lifetime, with tragic and irresolvable challenges. The difference between those who commit suicide in the face of such difficulties and those who weather the storm is the capacity to connect to others, to derive solace (and perhaps also material assistance) from a dense web of relationships to family, friends, and neighbors. His fear is that occupational differentiation unravels this web of connection. In his empirical work, he shows how suicide rates differ by groups and how these differences in rates reveal gaps in the social fabric. For instance, Durkheim certainly understood that even in a pluralistic world, poor people had fewer choices—especially fewer good choices—than others. Yet, poverty per se was not necessarily a predictor of suicide as suicide rates also increase during periods of rapid economic growth (Blasca-Fontecilla, et al., 2012). It is not difficulty alone that predicts suicide, but difficulty (or even just change) accompanied by social isolation that predicts anomic suicide.

The lack of common ground with neighbors endangers not only individuals, but the community as a whole, according to Durkheim. When society becomes highly differentiated, when individuals lead an atomistic existence, when a common civic or religious ground erodes, we are faced with a mass society. Mass society is characterized by a strong central state at the top, relatively disengaged individuals at the bottom, and few mediating institutions between them. In this situation the central government is likely to create an ersatz common ground in nationalism.

Nationalism, Durkheim fears, tilts all too easily toward chauvinism and then toward war. Thus, even the authoritarian escape from overchoice leads to disaster.

Consider our present circumstances. We have all heard the arguments about "hidden persuaders" (Packard, 1980) who use sexual desire—overtly or covertly expressed—to sell products. But sex is not the only desire used to sell product. The quest for community is also enlisted in the service of desire, reflected in the circle of friends at a beach picnic holding the right brand of beer, or the Christmas tree ornament mirroring the soft drink of choice. Nationalism and patriotism have also been bent to the service of desire: the car that used to be "the heartbeat of America," the deodorant that replaces the torch held high by the Statue of Liberty. At the same time that neighborliness on an intimate scale and neighborliness writ large as patriotism are used to sell product, we are also engaged militarily in at least two small wars and earnestly contemplating a third war in the Middle East. Durkheim would not be surprised. The contemporary environment is one in which marketing may be called upon to sell not only products and lifestyles, but also political systems, candidates, and, ultimately, wars.

Together, the work of the major classical theorists of sociology might be summarized as follows: Human beings' sense of identity and community is socially constructed within a deeply flawed and problematic context; one in which both the things that divide us (class and occupational differences), and the things that unite us (a secularized Protestant work ethic, nationalism, patriotism and chauvinism), may prove dangerous to the survival of our species and the planet.

Overchoice is conceived differently by each of these theorists: for Cooley, Mead, and Gehlen overchoice signals a breakdown in our social capacity to make meaning, including agreements about what choices should be so routinized that we are spared sensory overload. Marx points out the cruelty of being lured into meaningless choices that benefit our exploiters but not ourselves. Durkheim thinks that external factors—the multiplicity of lifestyles produced by occupational specialization (and, by extension, produced also by class, race, gender, age, regional, religious, and ethnic differences)—confront us with a situation of perpetual overchoice. Weber emphasizes internalized factors; the experience of industrial labor (whether capitalist or socialist) tempts us with fantasies of total control, and hence sends us on a slippery path of self-inflicted overchoice.

Faced with such challenges, marketing, like every other form of socially organized activity, must find a way to direct choices toward social justice alongside our already potent desire for material plenty and control over our lives.

2.5 References

Alberghina, L., & Westerhoff, H. V. (2005). *Systems biology: Definitions and perspectives*. Berlin, Germany: Springer Verlag.

Auyang, S. Y. (1998). *Foundations of complex systems theories: In economics, evolutionary biology, and statistical physics.* Cambridge, England: Cambridge University Press.

Barker, R. (1978). *Habits, environments, and human behavior.* San Francisco, CA: Jossey Bass.

Bateson, G. (1979). *Mind and nature: A necessary unity*. New York, NY: Bantam Books.

Becker, H. (1970). *Sociological work: Method and substance*. Chicago, IL: Aldine.

Berger, P., & Kellner, H. (1965). Arnold Gehlen and the theory of institutions. *Social Research*, 32(1), 110–115.

Berger, P., & Luckmann, T. (1966). *The social construction of reality.* New York, NY: Anchor Books.

Blasca-Fontecilla, H., Perez-Rodriguez, M., Garcia-Nieto, R., Fernandez-Navarro, P., Galfalvy, H., de Leon, J., & Baca-Garcia, E. (2012). Worldwide impact of economic cycles on suicide trends over 3 decades: Differences according to level of development. A mixed effects model study. *BMJ Open, 14*(May), 1-7.

Blumer, H. (1969). *Symbolic interactionism: Perspective and method.* Englewood Cliffs, NJ: Prentice-Hall.

Braverman, H. (1974). *Labor and monopoly capital.* New York, NY: Monthly Review Press.

Brunner, E., & Barth, K. (1946). *Natural theology: Comprising "nature and grace" and the reply "No!" by Karl Barth.* London, England: Centenary Press.

Brunner, K. (1996). Knowledge, values and the choice of economic organization. In T. Lys (Ed.), *Economic analysis and political ideology: The selected essays of Karl Brunner* (pp. 1-17) (Vol. 1). London, England: Elgar Publishers.

Burawoy, M. (1979). *Manufacturing consent: Changes in the labor process under monopoly Capitalism*. Chicago, IL: University of Chicago Press.

Burchill, S., Linkthaler, L., Devetak, R., Donnelly, J., Nardin, T., & Paterson, M. (2009). *Theories of international relations* (4th ed.). London, England: Palgrave.

Chinoy, E. (1955). *Automobile workers and the American dream*. New York, NY: Doubleday.

Conklin, D. W. (1991). *Comparative economic systems*. Calgary, Canada: University of Calgary Press.

Cooley, C. H. (1902). *Human nature and the social order.* New York, NY: Scribner's.

DeGreene, K. B., & Alluisi, E. A. (1970). *Systems psychology*. New York, NY: McGraw-Hill.

Diamond, S. (1971). The rule of law versus the order of custom. *Social Research, 38*(1), 42–72.

Durkheim, E. (1948). *The division of labor in society.* New York, NY: The Free Press. (Original work published 1893)

Durkheim, E. (1951). *Suicide.* Glencoe, IL: Free Press. (Original work published 1897)

Easton, D. (1965). *A systems analysis of political life*. New York, NY: Wiley.

Edwards, R. (1979). *Contested terrain: The transformation of the workplace in the twentieth century*. New York, NY: Basic Books.

Fromm, E. (1969). *Escape from freedom*. New York, NY: Holt, Rinehart and Winston.

Gehlen, A. (1988). *Man, his nature and place in the world.* New York, NY: Columbia University Press.

Gerth, H., & Mills, W. C. (1958). *From Max Weber.* New York, NY: Oxford University Press.

Gilder, G. (1993). *Wealth and poverty*. San Francisco, CA: ICS Press.

Grimm, J., & Grimm, W. (n.d.). *Little Snow White.* Retrieved from http://www.pitt.edu/~dash/type0709.html

Hein, M. (2011). Systemtheorie und Politik(wissenschaften)-Missverstandnis oder Produktive Herrausforderung? [Systems theory and politics/political science – Misunderstanding or productive challenge?]. In C. Gansel (Ed.),

Systemtheorie in Den Fachwissenschaften (pp. 53–77). Gottingen, Germany: Gottingen University Press.

Jacquemetton, A. (Writer), Jacquemetton, M. (Writer), & Manley, C. (Director). (2012). Commissions and fees [Television series episode]. In M. Weiner (Creator/Producer), *Mad Man*. Los Angeles, CA: AMC.

Kaneko, K. (2006). *Life: An introduction to complex systems biology*. Berlin, Germany: Springer Verlag.

Kaplan, M. A. (1968). Systems theory and political science. *Social Research, 35*, 30–47.

Locker, M. E. (2011). *Systems theory and theology: The living interplay between science and religion*. Eugene, OR: Wipf & Stock Publishers.

Maturano, H., & Varela, F. (1987). *The tree of knowledge: The biological roots of human understanding*. Boston, MA: Shambhala Publications.

McCartney, J. (1960). *Basic marketing: A managerial approach*. Homewood, IL: Richard Irwin, Inc.

Mead, G. H. (1956). *On social psychology*. Chicago, IL: University of Chicago Press.

National Institute of Occupational Safety and Health. (1997, July). *Plain language about shiftwork* [Report]. Cincinnatti, OH: National Institute of Occupational Safety and Health.

Omenn, G. S. (2006, December). Grand challenges and great opportunities in science, technology, and public policy. *Science, 314*, 1696–1704.

Packard, V. (1980). *The hidden persuaders*. New York, NY: Pocket Books.

Rosen, R. (1968). A means toward a new holism. *Science, 161*(July), 34–35.

Rowling, J. K. (1998). *Harry Potter and the sorcerer's stone*. New York, NY: A.A. Levine Books.

Samuelson, P. A., & Nordhaus, W. D. (2004). *Economics*. New York, NY: McGraw-Hill.

Snooks, G. (1999). *Global transition: A general theory of economic development*. London, England: Palgrave-Macmillan.

Spangler, E. (1992). Sexual harassment: Labor relations by other means? *New Solutions, 3*(1), 23–30.

Tausch, A., & Prager, F. (1993). *Towards a socio-liberal theory of world development*. New York, NY: McMillan/St. Martin.

Tucker, R. C. (1978). *The Marx-Engels reader* (2nd ed.). New York, NY, and London, England: W.W. Norton.

Weber, M. (1958). *The protestant ethic and the spirit of capitalism* (T. Parsons Trans.). New York, NY: Charles Scribner and Sons.

Wooding, J., & Levenstein, C. (1999). *The point of production: Work environment in advanced industrial societies*. New York, NY: Guilford Press.

Wright, E. O. (1985). *Classes*. London, England: Verso Books.

Yeung, K. T., & Martin, J. L. (2003). The looking glass self: An empirical test and elaboration. *Social Forces, 81*(3), 843–879.

CHAPTER III

Overchoice and the Future of Economic Thought

Erik E. Guzik

3.1 Introduction

If the central assumptions of mainstream economic theory are correct, overchoice should not exist. To state this another way, if overchoice is indeed a reality confronting individual consumers in the marketplace, then the current beliefs, assumptions, and market models underlying modern economic thought must be reconsidered.

Mainstream economic thought—often referred to as neoclassical theory—suggests that the primary economic problem facing the consumer, and the unmitigated problem against which individuals struggle in their lifelong quest for satisfaction, is material scarcity. Consumer wants are without limit, the theory goes, while available resources needed to satisfy those wants, are, by nature, limited. Our existence as consumers, then, is one worthy of timeless and classic stories of unrequited individual desire and unfulfilled dreams. Our economic lives are marked by painful, difficult choices as we seek to satisfy our unlimited want for material economic gain on the path toward ever greater satisfaction, yet we can never realize complete material and psychological satisfaction given the limits on resources we face inherently as maximizing economic agents.

According to the findings of overchoice, however, the basic plot of this story is misplaced, and the characters miscast. The primary struggle faced by the modern consumer is not facing too few options, but too many. The issue is not a scarcity of material output, but a surplus. The main challenge facing the individual consumer, then, is not rationally calculating the additional satisfaction of the limited consumption opportunities that present themselves, but the irrational dissatisfaction and inherent difficulty that arises naturally from facing an abundance of material opportunities (Ariely, 2008; Schwartz, 2004).

Certainly disagreements over the relevance of maximizing tendencies, scarcity, and individual choice are not new in economics, underlying the theoretical and policy contributions of Keynes, Veblen, Polanyi, Malthus, and a host of others throughout the history of economic thought. Further, the possibility of overchoice is not the only example of how modern economic thought seems to overlook basic economic realities in its simplifying models of individual behavior (see Wolff & Resnick, 2012).

However, overchoice brings into much sharper focus the increasing dissonance between modern economic theory and the current realities of consumer behavior. The possibility of an overload of choices for the individual—with attendant psychological discomfort and disutility—cuts into the very microfoundations of modern economic theory, including the assumed psychological behaviors, actions, and satisfactions of the individual economic actor as relating to the act of consumption (Botti & McGill, 2006; Iyengar & Lepper, 2000; Schwartz, 2004). Recent findings and insights in behavioral economics and neuroeconomics now threaten the very conceptualization of the individual agent—and the role of agency—in modern economic thought, especially involving our understanding into how resources might be produced, distributed, and consumed most effectively in the economy.

The purpose of this chapter is to analyze the assumptions of neoclassical economic theory as they relate to the main conclusions of overchoice. While some assumptions within current microeconomic models can withstand the ongoing and relentless onslaught of research findings from behavioral economics, neuroeconomics, and neuroscience itself regarding overchoice, this chapter believes other assumptions simply cannot; among these are assumptions of perfect competition and the perceived individual motivation of the rational economic agent, not only in terms of maximizing consumption behavior, as many critics have persuasively argued, but also the underlying determinants of the manifold, differentiated output facing overwhelmed consumers. As such, this chapter explores how the reality of overchoice connects not only to the modern consumer in the economy, but also the modern producer, further extending the concept of overchoice from the world of demand to that of supply.

Throughout, this chapter accepts the reality of overchoice qua product differentiation and its complex individual and social effects, and seeks to explain this reality by departing from conventional economic beliefs about the individual, individual motivations, and resultant market competition. The existence of overchoice suggests a remapping and reconceptualization of the microfoundations of economics, including the behaviors underlying individual agents of production and consumption. Policy arising from such beliefs, too, must likely be modified to better accommodate a more realistic set of economic assumptions. In particular, this chapter suggests that the existence of so-called "imperfect" market structures—market types that dominate the modern economic landscape—likely arise as a consequence of overchoice. This chapter also focuses on individual creativity within the spheres of consumption and production—referred to in this chapter as "economic creativity"—as a key consideration necessary to better understand the reality of human agency and overchoice, and how economics must begin to incorporate creativity as a foundational economic act into its theoretical arsenal in order to develop a richer understanding of economic motivation and outcomes at the levels of individual, firm, industry, and society.

3.2 Overchoice and the Main Assumptions of Neoclassical Theory

As traditionally defined, overchoice refers to an excess or surplus of options facing the consumer (Schwartz et al., 2002). The concept is often directly connected to individual cognition, specifically the inability of consumers to make efficient decisions in the midst of an overload of options (Iyengar, Jiang, & Huberman, 2004). One of the most penetrating insights of neuroeconomics is therefore that individuals may not be driven by maximizing behavior as they make decisions regarding consumption, falling back on "irrational" heuristics (Ariely, 2008).

This chapter begins by exploring the main assumptions of neoclassical theory as related to the consumer and consumer choice. The chapter explores how neoclassical theory constructs an understanding of consumer utility and value based on expected satisfaction of articles of consumption. In so doing, the chapter lays the groundwork for an examination of the relevance of neoclassical theory's main assumptions of consumer behavior given findings within overchoice theory.

3.3 Consumers, Utility, and Value

As many theorists of overchoice have noted, one defining element of neoclassical theory is its unique conceptualization of the individual, especially as involving the act of consumption. Consumer behavior is assumed to be driven by material interests, including an inherent desire for more (Iyengar, Jiang, & Huberman, 2004; Reutskaja & Hogarth, 2009). Within microeconomic models, for instance, consumer behavior is defined by non-satiation, the idea that consumers hold boundless material wants and can therefore never be truly satisfied.

Hence, animating the individual as an economic agent within neoclassical models is a type of deterministic behavior, as the consumer attempts to accumulate an ever greater quantum of material wealth with the objective of obtaining material and psychological satisfaction. Though recent revisions within neoclassical theory—some appearing in response to new and growing findings in psychology, biology, and neuroscience—have attempted to repaint this reductionist notion of individual self-interest, they extend beyond simple materialistic maximizing behavior. The basic assumption of maximization nevertheless remains, underpinning important principles within its basic economic models, including its constituent and defining laws of demand and supply, as well as conclusions about partial and general market equilibrium.

Interestingly, this unwavering belief in individual maximizing behavior is likely a self-imposed (and, this chapter argues, self-defeating) caricature of human behavior within many microeconomic models. Certainly, foundational schools of thought that preceded the appearance of classical and neoclassical theory in economics, including especially mercantilist thought, held strong to the idea of wealth maximization as the *sine qua non* of individual economic behavior and self-interest. Bernard Mandeville, for instance, likely shaped by Western religion's conception of material gain at the time, did indeed argue persuasively that individuals maximized utility via ongoing wealth accumulation. Mandeville defined individual economic interests as driven by the limitless acquisitive appetite and the boundless desire for gain, the pursuit of which, in Mandeville's view (and contra contemporaneous moralist teachings), helped drive material progress and development (Mandeville, 1962).

However, Adam Smith and other classical economists criticized strongly and repeatedly the notion that individuals are driven solely by materialistic interests. In his *Theory of Moral Sentiments*, Smith (1790) noted that individuals are motivated by a number of non-material interests, many of which detract from material accumulation. Hume and Selby (1902) also noted that self-interest as a sole determinant of human behavior, was, as in Mandeville's view, a "fancied monster." Taken in context, such views can hardly be considered surprising. Smith and Hume very consciously saw themselves as battling the dominant mercantilist ideas and policies of their time, including Mandeville's "fancied monster" of self-interest.

Modern models of individual behavior and maximization, too, differ sometimes markedly from those originally introduced by the foundational mercantilist school centuries ago. Indeed, within neoclassical theory, consumer behavior takes a very interesting and nuanced form which involves the actual attempts of the consumer to maximize satisfaction. As an example, consider the notion of value as it relates to consumer utility. From the perspective of neoclassical economics, market price is an important measure of the consumer's willingness to pay for a good or service, derived from the additional utility that is expected to appear during the act of consumption. Within consumer behavior models, however, additional amounts of consumer utility do not remain the same as consumption of a good continues, nor do they increase.

Indeed, as the marginalist school of economics explained in the late nineteenth century, when an individual consumes more of any good, there is a relative decrease in satisfaction or utility realized from each additional unit of consumption. Indeed, the marginalists modified dramatically and expanded the idea of consumer utility and value beyond that introduced by the mercantilist and classical schools, illustrating that greater consumption of homogenous product leads to concomitant and incremental decreases in utility and value. In more common language, as a product is consumed increasingly, it loses value in the mind of the individual consumer. Within neoclassical models, then, *more is not necessarily better for the consumer.*

In fact, the more of any particular good consumed, the less additional utility the consumer receives.

Though some have attacked neoclassical theory based on the idea that marginal utility is never allowed to become negative within its consumer behavior models, no matter the level of consumption, such criticism misses the key contribution of the marginalists in understanding the consumer's unique demand for original and differentiated output. The consumer's reaction to common, trite and ordinary output is clear—subjective consumer value falls as the consumption of homogenous output increases.

This basic understanding of consumer satisfaction, today referred to as the principle of diminishing marginal utility, is a defining element of neoclassical consumer theory. Diminishing utility strongly suggests that the value placed on new and different types of goods springs from innate consumer preference. This basic behavioral phenomena—diminishing satisfaction with common and expected options, that is, *a lack of choice and variation*—seems to describe how consumers place value on a large variety of goods and services in the modern economy, including clothing, entertainment, music, and fast food. From this perspective, product differentiation in modern markets is likely secured by important demand considerations that have been neglected heretofore in overchoice theory (as well as, this chapter notes below, within contemporary microeconomic studies of markets and product differentiation).

At this point, it is important to highlight that some central elements of modern microeconomics may not be so removed from recent findings within overchoice theory as some have assumed. In fact, one might argue that any apparent dissonance between neoclassical theory and the realities of overchoice may be resolved by undertaking a deeper, more focused look into the microfoundations of the individual consumer within neoclassical theory, especially as relating to the principle of falling marginal utility. The issue is worth further examination, as many criticisms levied by overchoice theory against microeconomics are likely sound, while others are not, as least according to the nuanced understanding of consumer behavior presented within many micro models.

For instance, central to contemporary utility theory and the concept of diminishing marginal utility is the principle of rational choice. That is, individuals face ceaseless choices qua consumers, especially given diminishing marginal utility and their limited consumptive resources (income). In this situation, consumers maximize total utility by choosing a basket of goods based on calculations of marginal utility received from different products and services as each additional dollar of income is spent.

In short, one might see the neoclassical principle of rational choice as itself founded on the very notion and possibility of choice overload, as the consumer must maximize utility based on a choice set that is greater than available individual resources. That is, consumers are forced to maximize utility based on commodity choice precisely because available options outweigh consumer resources. Add in heterogeneous preferences showcased by different consumers, and the appearance of manifold options in the marketplace may not be all that surprising.

Certainly, viewing the assumptions of neoclassical theory in this way to accommodate the existence of overchoice does seem to provide a potential solution to the problem at hand, explaining why, for instance, an individual consumer might choose a subcompact auto over a sport pickup truck. Yet, even with such conceptual contortions, this solution fails to explain why multiple sport pickups, differentiated and branded in myriad ways in the modern auto industry, appear in the first place (a market reality discussed in more detail below).

Moreover, as critics of rational choice note, overchoice suggests that consumers do not benefit, but rather suffer from such large and open-ended choice sets, and are often rendered incapable of making efficient choices in the face of a multitude of options. Finally, if resolving the incongruities between modern economic thought and the realities of overchoice depends on accepting the idea of material abundance (with manifold output variations and options) in the economy, then material scarcity is not an underlying issue in the modern economy after all, or the concept of scarcity means something very different than what is currently believed in the field of economics.

3.4 Markets and Economic Efficiency

An important conclusion that follows from the conceptualization of the individual within neoclassical theory is that of consumer sovereignty. Efficient forms of production, according to neoclassical models, must ultimately respond to the specific needs and wants of the individual consumer, lest productive inefficiency and waste appear in the economy and diminish potential consumption opportunities.

According to neoclassical principles, the market structure that best responds to this basic requirement of maximal consumer demand is pure (often called perfect) competition. That is, a market defined by the following set of basic characteristics: a very large number of small producers, homogeneous output, and complete information for buyers and sellers.

According to models of pure competition, firms in each industry respond without restriction to consumer need, free to enter and exit each market as required to maximize consumer utility and short-run economic profit. Further, given pure competition, constituent firms within each industry produce identical forms of output, resulting in a long-run equilibrium defined to be economically efficient: that is, output price within each market is just equal to average costs of production for participating firms. Neoclassical theory argues that the consumer ultimately benefits from pure competition, as competitive pressures prevent prices from rising above production costs in long-run microeconomic models, allowing for greater material consumption. To see this, note that if prices were to rise above average costs, the total consumption of wealth would necessarily decrease for buyers.

One key to efficient outcomes in pure competition, then, is the inclusion of the assumption of homogenous product. Indeed, if firms were to innovate in the form of product variation, such actions would create a monopoly position for the innovating firm. Though temporary, this monopoly position would allow prices to rise above average intra-industry costs (given the momentary absence of competition), much to the detriment of the end consumer (technically, consumer surplus falls within microeconomic models describing this situation). The model of pure competition therefore envisions an ideal and efficient world as one marked by imitation, not innovation.

Hence, from the perspective of overchoice, one obvious shortcoming of existing models of pure competition is not only the idea of individual maximizing behavior (that is, the consumer is assumed to always prefer more to less), but also the absence of any product variation and difference within markets. That is, if overchoice is an accurate description of current economic and social phenomena, then a slightly more realistic depiction of the toothpaste market would require that the different types of toothpaste offered therein to be some number greater than one.

To be sure, microeconomics recognizes this possibility of product variation beyond what appears in pure competition. To understand differentiation by firms within markets, microeconomic theory introduces what it considers to be "impure" or "inefficient" market forms. Typically, three imperfect markets are explored in resultant micro models: monopoly, oligopoly, and monopolistic competition. In relation to overchoice, the most relevant of these imperfect market structures may be monopolistic competition, though, as this chapter argues below, the existence of monopoly and oligopoly may be based in no small measure on the consumer preference for limited product options as suggested by overchoice theory.

Like pure competition, monopolistic competition is defined by numerous, small firms, and their free entry and exit into markets. However, in stark contrast to pure competition, producers within monopolistic competition compete for consumers and market share based on differentiated rather than homogeneous output.

Given product differentiation within monopolistic competition, firms realize temporary monopoly prices via prices that rise above average costs within an industry. The result is short term profitability, the ongoing existence of which depends on continuing innovation on the part of the firm. According to this model of production, then, the social act of competition spurs monopolistic competitors to innovate, illustrating the net impact of market competition on product differentiation, and the concomitant negative impact on the consumer. From the perspective of neoclassical theory, therefore, product differentiation and innovation comes with a hefty price—the loss of consumer surplus, and with it, market efficiency.

Product markets marked by monopolistic competition, this chapter believes, present a thorny issue for both modern microeconomics and overchoice theory. First, it is interesting to note that overchoice theory generally agrees with the conclusions drawn by neoclassical theory regarding market efficiency and product differentiation. Too much choice within a market (what is now deemed intra-market choice) is indeed an issue within both positions. For neoclassical theory, any intra-market choice generates economic inefficiency and a loss of consumer satisfaction. Overchoice theory likewise suggests that too many options lead to consumer disutility and suboptimal decision-making. Hence, the findings of overchoice per se do not cut against the assumptions of neoclassical theory regarding the impact on consumer behavior and decision-making, at least as they relate to monopolistic competition.

Further, the existence of monopolistic competition and product differentiation strongly suggest that consumers do in fact value options, variety, and choice; at least within some important subsets of industries and markets. It is perhaps tempting to reduce resultant product variation and novelty to supply-side determinants—product differentiation and choice that appears against the true wishes of the consumer. Yet the notions of consumer sovereignty and diminishing marginal utility, especially as they relate to consumer demand and preference for the unique and original—in short, the desire for product difference—cannot be dismissed so easily.

3.5 An Initial Theoretical Resolution

Economics now requires new understandings of value based on the novelty of output and new methods of illustrating consumer benefit within "imperfect" market structures. For instance, within monopolistic competition, the greater utility offered by differentiated products can be understood to offset the higher output price consumers pay for unique output. In other words, consumers are revealing their preference and willingness to pay for the novelty and product differentiation generated within monopolistic competition. There is no loss of consumer surplus in such cases, as variety and differentiation are part and parcel of satisfying consumer demand adequately within these particular market structures.

Further, it is interesting to consider how product differentiation and overchoice might connect to other types of "imperfect" market structures beyond monopolistic competition. Though monopoly (one producer) and oligopoly (a few producers) are often understood within basic microeconomic models to appear within markets defined by barriers to competition, it may be that these variant market structures arise in response to important differences in consumer choice relative to products and entire industries. That is, consumer preferences regarding choice may provide important conditions securing certain market structures (monopoly and oligopoly) and not others (monopolistic competition) within particular industries. In short, monopoly and oligopoly may be more likely to appear in markets defined by a desired, limited consumer choice set (oil, gas, cigarettes, etc.), whereas monopolistic competition may appear in markets (pharmaceuticals, fashion, mobile applications, etc.) driven by the desire of consumers for greater variety and choice.

If this line of reasoning is sound, then the price premium firms realize within monopoly and oligopoly, as in the case of monopolistic competition, may not be the result of productive inefficiency, but may rather reflect the value and preference consumers place on facing a limited set of options, as suggested by overchoice theory. That is, if there is indeed benefit for the consumer in facing limited options, the resultant market structure defining an industry may reveal this social preference, and price may likewise reflect the differential changes in utility consumers realize when facing a more limited set of choices than that offered in pure competition. That oligopoly is a dominant form of market competition in most advanced industrial societies therefore rests in part on the preference (or, at the very least, the acceptance) of consumers of a delimited set of choices involving such products as cigarettes, soda, and cereal. A similar argument might be offered for the oligopoly in resource and capital markets.

3.6 Economic Creativity

Production differentiation—and resultant consumer choice—this chapter argues, holds a very important connection to economic creativity. Creativity is now cited increasingly as a key condition for sustained innovation in business—the true stuff of magic for large, global companies like Toyota, Intel, and Apple. And creativity is no less important for the myriad coffee shops, sandwich shops, printing shops, etc., that depend on differentiation and micro-markets for their continued existence in small towns and cities alike.

Ironically, however, the magic stuff of economic creativity is not studied in micro economics. For instance, within most introductory textbooks of microeconomics, the term creativity does not appear as an index entry. Likewise, there is no chapter on creativity within such textbooks, and certainly no textbook on the microfoundations of creativity. Indeed, in most introductory texts, the concept of creativity only appears, if at all, passingly at the end of the text during discussion of the "impure" or "imperfect" market structure of monopolistic competition. Further, the term does not appear at all within advanced and graduate levels of microeconomics, and it is not analyzed as a foundational element of consumption and production. Hence, while there is strong and growing interest, especially in business, concerning issues involving regional and national innovation systems and creative classes, all are comfortably situated in the domain of macroeconomic analysis, with scant notice from current microeconomic models and microeconomic theory.

Ironically perhaps, this chapter must then borrow from a definition of creativity forged in the domain of psychology: creativity is the ability to produce something novel that holds value. For the purpose of this chapter, creativity, then, entails the ability to produce new (differentiated) output that embodies value for some end consumer, and is therefore of central importance to understand the existence of overchoice.

When applied in the economy, creativity separates market leaders from everyone else. Economic creativity is the source of new product ideas, new product features, new advertising slogans, new production methods, new cost saving methods, and entirely new markets. Economic creativity not only enhances the production of value, in many cases, it *is the* production of value. Further, if models of diminishing marginal utility and monopolistic competition are accurate descriptions of reality, which this chapter believes they are, *economic creativity is furthermore secured by consumer preferences.*

That the two main concepts defining creativity according to psychologists (production and value) are central to the domain of economics should perhaps indicate its relevance to a field of study that claims interest in supply and demand. Of note, the notion of "man the creator" (often referred to as *homo faber*) has been an important contribution throughout the history of economic thought by those who have wished to push the future of economic theory in more realistic and useful directions. This conception of individual economic behavior also helps to explain the reality of overchoice as it relates to product differentiation.

In the case of monopolistic competition, the creation and realization of social value is likely the underlying motivation of the individual creator, and by extension, the appearance of product differentiation within certain market structures. Given such "imperfect" forms of competition, we can perhaps understand why innovative firms not only introduce new and different products, but also why advertising tries to convince the consumer that such products are indeed "new and improved," even if this is not truly the case. Within monopolistic competition, firms produce differentiated output with few substitutes, connecting uniquely with the consumer's desire for difference and variation. The wants of the consumer for greater variety are answered by the ability of firms to satisfy this unique demand.

This chapter certainly does not mean to boil down overchoice to a new form of maximization—the demand of consumers for ever-greater difference. The consumer demand for differentiated products is likely complex and perhaps contradictory. Indeed, even within monopolistic competition, demand for differentiated products may be a reaction by the consumer to overchoice. That is, product differentiation may provide the overwhelmed consumer with a novel shortcut for dealing with a plethora of common and overwhelming choices. Differentiation provides a reduced set of options within an otherwise unwieldy grouping of consumption possibilities, relieving consumers of the burden of making additional product comparisons. In short, the claim of "new and improved" may provide a valuable aid to consumers who might otherwise have no recourse in choosing between otherwise indistinguishable options. Economic creativity and resultant product differentiation, this chapter therefore argues, may provide the overwhelmed buyer with a novel solution—increasingly, consumers demand the new and unique (the uncommon) as a response against too many common options. In a similar manner, Iyengar (2010) suggests that one way consumers might deal with overchoice is product categorization. In this case, the category of "new and improved" can grant the consumer a novel escape from the overchoice dilemma.

This conclusion may likewise help to explain the seeming paradox of overchoice within some markets (again, intra-market choice), but not others. That is, if consumers are affected negatively by overchoice, then why do producers create such variation in the first place? Research and development is certainly a cost for firms. So is advertising. If consumer sovereignty is a driving economic activity, firms should seek rationally to maximize consumer utility and value, and limit options (and therefore costs). Yet they do not, as the existence of overchoice and monopolistic competition make abundantly clear.

It would again seem tempting to derive product differentiation (and, by extension, overchoice) from the profit motive, as Schumpeter and others have done in their examination of product markets, again referring back to mercantilistic notion of individual maximizing behavior. Yet such solutions fail to recognize the key contribution of consumers in driving creativity, innovation, differentiation, and value in markets. They also fail to recognize the inherent desire of individuals to create, resulting in the product variation that appears within many key markets and industries in the modern economy.

3.7 Conclusions and Policy Implications

The potential connection between overchoice and imperfect market structures is an interesting one to consider. Consumer behavior is likely an underlying condition of product differentiation within markets defined by monopolistic competition, and is furthermore an important area of study within future overchoice research. If consumers did not demand differentiated output and manifold product options, monopolistic competitors would undoubtedly lack the markets required for their unique output.

Further, the unease and disutility that consumers face when confronted with too much choice involving certain products and markets may explain the appearance of monopoly and oligopoly in many segments of the modern economy. If such market structures are in fact formed, in part, in response to consumer demand for limited choice, they may not be economically inefficient, as currently concluded in microeconomic models, rather providing a unique solution to the disutility associated with overchoice.

Nevertheless, this chapter advances that the belief—common in overchoice theory—that consumers might benefit more from limited choice, with resultant policy implications, should be questioned. Consumer desire for product variation has resulted likely from the long historical advantage our species secured in seeking out and preferring variation and difference: different forms of shelter, different sources and types of food, different conceptualizations of problems, different solutions to identified problems, and so on. Our desire for the new and unique—that is, product differentiation—has most likely not only served us well in our evolutionary development as a species, but also animates such market structures as monopolistic competition in the modern economy.

Nevertheless, the reality of overchoice and product differentiation suggests the need for a new way to think of self-interest and individual behavior in microeconomics. As noted above, we have long believed in microeconomics in the idea of non-satiation. Yet human behavior seems marked not so much by a desire for more, but rather a desire for greater difference and variation as part and parcel of the act of consumption. Together with the innate desire of individuals to create wealth and diversity, product differentiation can no longer be considered as an anomaly of economic life, *but rather one of its most defining and central conditions.* Our "self-interest" as individual producers and consumers seems to rest not so much on the chase of wealth, but rather on the manifold and varied forms of its creation, and the enjoyment that we receive from consuming such variations.

This reconceptualization of individual behavior and market types is important for future developments in the field of overchoice. The general belief that a distaste for differentiation and choice defines consumers is a difficult one to maintain, given current economic realities. It is much more likely that consumers' desire for the new and unique is dependent in part on the industry and market in question, helping to shape the particular macroeconomic form that each market takes.

3.8 References

Ariely, D. (2008). *Predictably irrational: The hidden forces that shape our decisions.* New York, NY: HarperCollins Publishers.

Botti, S., & McGill, A. L. (2006). When choosing is not deciding: The effect of perceived responsibility on satisfaction. *Journal of Consumer Research, 33*(2), 211–219.

Hume, D., & Selby-Bigge, L. A. (1902). *Enquiries concerning the human understanding: And concerning the principles of morals.* Oxford, England: Clarendon Press.

Iyengar, S. (2010). *The art of choosing.* New York, NY: Twelve, Hachette Book Group.

Iyengar, S., Jiang, W., & Huberman, G. (2004). How much choice is too much? Contributions to 401(k) retirement plans. In O. Mitchell & S. Utkus (Eds.), *Pension design and structure: New lessons from behavioral finance* (pp. 83-96). Oxford, England: Oxford University Press.

Iyengar, S., & Lepper, M. R. (2000). When choice is demotivating: Can one desire too much of a good thing? *Journal of Personality and Social Psychology, 79*(6), 995–1006.

Mandeville, B. (1962). The grumbling hive; Or, knaves turn'd honest. In I. Primer (Ed.), *The fable of the bees: Private vices, public benefits* (pp. 27-38). New York, NY: Capricorn Books.

Reutskaja, E., & Hogarth, R. M. (2009). Satisfaction in choice as a function of the number of alternatives: When "goods satiate." *Psychology & Marketing, 26*(3), 197–202.

Schwartz, B. (2004). *The paradox of choice: Why more is less.* New York, NY: Harper Collins.

Schwartz, B., Ward, A., Monterosso, J., Lyubomirsky, S., White, K., & Lehman, D.R. (2002). Maximizing versus satisficing: Happiness is a matter of choice. *Journal of Personality and Social Psychology, 83*(5), 1178–1197.

Smith, A. (1790). *The theory of moral sentiments*. London, England: A. Millar.

Wolff, R. D., & Resnick, S. A. (2012). *Contending economic theories*. Cambridge, MA: M.I.T. Press.

CHAPTER IV

Consumer Information Overload

Perspectives from Consumer Culture Theory and Experience Marketing

Stefano Pace

4.1 Introduction

We live in an information society. Whenever we use our smartphone to check our profile on our preferred social networking site, our screen fills with a flow—or overflow—of images, data, and texts. This overflow of information also relates to our lives as consumers. Consumption is an activity that defines our lifestyle and a considerable part of our self. Consumption entails selecting from different alternatives, weighing options, and choosing. All these activities taken together, and even the single consumption choice itself, may make it necessary to manage information overload.

This chapter provides a cursory overview of how consumer culture views consumer information overload. Compared to traditional cognitive approaches, consumer culture theory (Arnould & Thompson, 2005, 2015) may provide a different perspective on how consumers experience an excessive flow of information.

Consumer culture is a "social arrangement in which the relations between lived culture and social resources, and between meaningful ways of life and the symbolic and material resources on which they depend, are mediated through markets" (Arnould & Thompson, 2015, p. 19). Through consumer culture theory and its streams of analysis, we can approach information overload by exploring research paths, such as communities and assemblage theory. In addition, the experiential marketing approach provides a perspective on consumer overload.

In the following section this chapter synthesizes some of the typical dimensions through which the concept of information overload is presented. Then, the chapter illustrates how different streams of research within consumer culture theory can provide a new understanding for these overload dimensions. Finally, this chapter discusses the role of the consumption experience—a research stream that has some connections to consumer culture theory, but which also developed independently from this theory—as a means through which consumers can reduce the burden of choice.

4.2 The Dimensions of Choice Overload

The discourse of consumer overchoice revolves around the three major topics of products (goods and services that contain attributes which are very complex and very rich), markets (markets are flooded with assortments of products that are too broad), and consumer psychology (the consumer's brain cannot process too much information or it is trapped in some form of biased decision). Following is a more detailed discussion of these three topics.

1. Products become more and more complex. Electronic devices such as smartphones have many options, apps, and functions. Some of this complexity is due to competition, as competing companies add more and more features and options to their offers to gain more market share. Other sources of complexity are expressed through regulations, which, in cases such as food products, require the manufacturers to provide information and sophisticated specifications on a label to enable an informed product decision by the consumer and avoid any possible risk of misunderstanding or misalignment between the producer and the consumer. For example, detailed labels with information about allergens,

place of production, and packaging materials now accompany food products. Despite the fact that these are important pieces of information, they might also create some overload in the mind of the consumer.

Product attributes can be classified as alignable or nonalignable (Gourville & Soman, 2005; Markman & Medin, 1995; Zhang & Markman, 1998). Alignable attributes are easy to compare, and therefore they do not create a challenge for the consumer. For instance, a smartphone with an eight-inch display is comparable to a smartphone with a seven-inch display. On the other hand, nonalignable attributes are not easy to compare. A smartphone with a pop-up keyboard cannot be compared easily to a smartphone that has a powerful antenna.

2. Markets show the variety of the attributes a product possesses through brand assortments. Compared to a brand with a smaller assortment, a brand with a wider assortment of products is generally thought to be more attractive to consumers. Yet, the type of assortment is as relevant as its width (the number of closely-related product items a company offers). In fact, an increase in the assortment of nonalignable attributes increases the cognitive effort the consumer must undertake when choosing a product, in turn increasing the possibility of decision regret (Gourville & Soman, 2005). When the attributes are alignable, the consumer must decide which features the consumer considers relevant. In the case of purchasing a car, for example, a consumer might consider fuel economy, number of doors, or the speed of the car. These features make relative decision levels quite transparent (e.g., a speed of 120 miles per hour is different than a speed of 80 miles per hour). When facing a comparison among nonalignable features, the consumer should refer to advanced, and thus more complex, decision criteria, such as product utility or personal preferences. The consumer should decide, for example, whether an apartment with a rooftop is better than a house with a nice interior—two non-comparable features presenting an "all or nothing" dilemma; if the consumer chooses the rooftop, the consumer does not get the beautiful interior. This move toward a more elaborate decision criterion puts the consumer in a state of uneasiness and complexity that may cause the consumer to defer the decision or to not choose at all.

3. Psychologically, if a consumer faces a wide range of product alternatives, they experience a conflict, especially if many of these alternatives have different advantages and disadvantages (Tversky & Shafir, 1992). This state of conflict generates frustration and causes the consumer to defer the actual decision. After the choice has been made, there is also a higher probability that the consumer will regret a purchase decision (Iyengar & Lepper, 2000).

4.3 The Effects of Consumer Communities on Choice Overload

When consumers feel that the locus of a decision is inside themselves (internal locus of control), the positive or negative effects caused by the outcome of an event (a decision made) are increased. Conversely, if the locus of control is perceived as external to the self, the responses to the decision are less intense. Therefore, when one personally chooses an outcome, as opposed to the outcome is chosen for one by someone else "generates more intense emotional responses because of the greater sense of personal causality associated with choice" (Botti & McGill, 2011, p. 1066). When the subject is part of a consumer community (Cova, 1997; Muñiz & O'Guinn, 2001), this belonging can have some effects on the choice overload consumers feel. Communities are characterized by a sense of "we-intention" (Bagozzi & Dholakia, 2002), which is a common feeling of unity that provides individuals with a sense that they are part of the community and that the community creates their identity. This sense of we-ness encourages subjects to take collective actions and act as a group. The sense of we-ness can alleviate negative feelings caused by an overwhelming decision thanks to the shared responsibility of making that decision. When choosing in a community, the consumer relies on the rest of the group and on its shared norms, thus easing the burden the individual feels. The locus of control is partially external and, therefore, does not cause the heightened effect that can result from choosing by oneself.

On the other hand, a community may also cause choice overload. Consumer communities are formed by expert consumers who can share the extensive knowledge and passion they have about a product (experience). Fans of the Mini Cooper car, for instance, can create a repository of knowledge about the car—for example, its history, different model types, and technical details—that expands the scope of any single Mini Cooper fan's knowledge. Consuming the brand may become an extenuating exercise of showing one's expertise and taste to the community. This phenomenon of community-induced complexity would increase the choice overload for the single consumer. However, a mature community can also create solutions to this kind of overload problem. In a community, experienced consumers usually assume a specific, yet informal, role with clear tasks. For instance, the fan community of a particular motion picture might include consumers who are recognized experts about the history of the movie. These consumers do not need to acquire the entire knowledge the community possesses about the movie (e.g., knowledge about actors, screenplays, box office data) to attain the same status and acknowledgment as expert-members of the movie group. Even though the community generates a significant amount of knowledge, the assignment of different roles to community members ensures that information overload is kept at bay.

4.4 Assemblage Theory and Information Overload

Assemblage theory is an autonomous theoretical approach and a recent addition to the topics studied in consumer culture theory. Assemblage theory has some roots in practice theory (Reckwitz, 2002) and actor-network theory (Latour, 2005). It argues that heterogeneous elements can form coherent systems. By realizing that a unified whole is made up of elements that originate from different sources and are of different nature, the observer can gain a deeper understanding of the dynamics that characterize the object of inquiry. As a case in point, consumer communities are networks that connect objects, products, and individuals (Chambers, Price, & Schau, 2013). Entire conceptualizations can be created from the assemblage of elements. How surfers think about the concept of nature, for example, is an assemblage of technologies (such as the surfboard and surf clothing) and the knowledge of natural elements (such as winds, weather forecasts, and beach locations) (Canniford & Shankar, 2013). Surfers have to maintain constantly this assemblage through purifying practices—practices through which consumers expel the inconsistencies or contradictions of the assemblage—thereby demonstrating the fragility of the assemblage of nature (Canniford & Shankar, 2013). Therefore, consumers reassemble the pristine quality of the natural surfing environment by, for instance, introducing simpler surfing practices and materials that are less technology-driven into the assemblage. To experience nature, consumers can create entire new markets by assembling different elements. For example, the minimoto—a minibike for children—was redesigned to be ridden and raced by adults (Martin & Schouten, 2014).

Applying assemblage theory to consumption may help to create an understanding for the information overload concept. Products are assemblages of different elements that sometimes form bundles of information which are too rich for the consumer to process. In the past, for example, mobile phones were made up of elements that, in their similarity to landline phones, were relatively easy to use. Today's smartphones are electronic devices that possess a great number of elements such as software constantly providing users with news alerts, social media apps (like Twitter) with which users engage in public discussions, social media apps (like Snapchat) used for private conversations, and a security discourse that touches on the use of phones to store sensitive data (see, for instance, the latest controversy between Apple and the FBI about unlocking iPhones to acquire personal information). The consumer is at the core of this clash between different technologies and discourses. The consumer has to try to keep all of the elements together when using a smartphone. Trying to keep all the elements together (assemblage) and maintaining the elements can place a burden on the consumer. In this case, the overload can be not only informational, but also emotional. For example, the user has to transition from the emoji of a casual conversation to the technical jargon of a serious business report. A sense of urgency and continuous attachment to the smartphone is required to maintain the assemblage that defines an electronic device. In this context, the smartphone market is an assemblage in itself. The discourses around a smartphone include, for instance, concerns about how to dispose of this electronic device and the effects of technology on young users. The smartphone is not the only product that represents an assemblage. The house and car markets, for example, are also assemblages that force consumers to face quite complex decisions, strike a fine balance between heterogeneous elements, and process the product consumption (logics). The overload can be unsustainable due to the nearly inevitable contradictions that these elements might have.

4.5 Consumption of Experience as a Mode for Complexity Reduction

A key contribution to the literature on consumer experience as related to information overload is the transition from a purely utilitarian view of customers to a more holistic view (Carù & Cova, 2007; Pine & Gilmore, 1999). In the utilitarian view, customers search for a mono-dimensional value based on the perceived rational utility that they would derive from a product. Information is the foundation customers use to evaluate the value that they can expect to receive from a market offer. On the contrary, the experience literature adds other dimensions of value, such as the hedonic (Holbrook & Hirschman, 1982), social, and aesthetic dimensions. In this case, value does not really have information. One may adopt a phenomenological view. In this view, experiences "are usually internal, subjective, event-specific, and context-specific" (Helkkula, 2011, p. 375). Value is the lived experience embedded in the life-world of the consumer (Helkkula & Kelleher, 2010). Therefore, information overload is not possible because information is not the core element of the experience.

Other forms of excesses or overflow are possible. Following the classification of experience as suggested by Lanier and Rader (2015), some types of experience take the form of adventures. These are experiences based on the idea of the *ilinx*—a temporary disruption of one's perception through over-stimulation of the senses, similar to the feeling of dizziness and disorientation one experiences during a vertigo episode (Caillois, 2001). These experiences search for the unexpected and engage with the uncertainty of existence. These experiences may have some degree of excess and overflow. However, in this case, there is no information processing as it occurs in rational consumers in a neoclassical sense. In addition, the experience literature emphasizes ordinary experiences (Carù & Cova, 2003) as opposed to extraordinary ones. Ordinary experiences usually do not have over-stimulating effects. In this context, information overload is not really at the center of this discussion.

In order to understand consumer overload, one can also refer to the model of experience appropriation (Carù & Cova, 2006). When consumers face a new consumption experience, they adopt strategies of experience appropriation. The "operations of appropriation are the mark of a fundamental psychological system of action on the context of experience in order to transform and personalise it. These subjective operations hang together in allowing consumers to reduce the distance that can exist between them and the context of experience and so on, to facilitate immersion in the experience" (Carù & Cova, 2006, p. 6). In short, consumers customize and personalize experiences to make them their own and manageable. One can see appropriations as operations through which consumers reduce the complexity of the experience. It is a complexity based not only on information, but also on sensations and how the product is perceived. The possible overload is filtered through the process of appropriation in order for the individual to become familiar with the experience and enjoy it.

4.6 Conclusions

Typically, cognitive psychology is the primary theoretical source used to guide discussions about information overload. The discussion in this chapter attempted to provide a different way of looking at consumer information overload. This different approach, namely that of consumer culture theory combined with experience marketing, may contribute to a new conceptualization of overload. This conceptualization has some interesting implications for managers and companies.

First, managers might want to view their products and services as assemblages of different logics and elements. By observing the consumer's actual use of the product, the company can discover any difficulties that might arise through this assemblage and then provide solutions. For instance, a car sharing service is an assemblage of concepts such as sharing, renting, car-pooling, non-ownership, and their related tangible and intangible elements. The company can simplify its overall service concept by emphasizing just one of the sub-concepts (such as renting), so that the user can adopt a single logic to approach the service while discovering the others during the product usage. For example, a customer can use a car sharing service by just renting the service, thus simplifying their initial consumption, and then can discover the idea of product-sharing. Product-sharing is a new way of using goods and services and a way of reducing one's ecological footprint.

Second, in order to avoid overloading their customers, managers should not consider information as the only data source for consumers. To prevent overloading, experience marketing suggests that consumption, if seen as an experience, is a source that can create different stimuli for consumers. These stimuli may cause an overload. However, consumers are able to use the processes of familiarization and appropriation to organize this complexity. Managers should support consumers in this process by trying to understand how consumers arrange their consumption.

4.7 References

Arnould, E. J., & Thompson, C. J. (2005). Consumer Culture Theory (CCT): Twenty years of research. *Journal of Consumer Research, 31*(March), 868–882.

Arnould, E. J., & Thompson, C. J. (2015). Consumer Culture Theory: Ten years gone (and beyond). In A. Thyroff, J. B. Murray, & R. W. Belk (Eds.), *Research in consumer behavior* (Vol. 17). Bingley, England: Emerald Group Publishing.

Bagozzi, R. P., & Dholakia, U. M. (2002). Intentional social actions in virtual communities. *Journal of Interactive Marketing, 16*(2), 2–21.

Botti, S., & McGill, A. L. (2011). The locus of choice: Personal causality and satisfaction with hedonic and utilitarian decisions. *Journal of Consumer Research, 37*(6), 1065–1078.

Caillois, R. (2001). *Man, play, and games.* Champaign, IL: University of Illinois Press.

Canniford, R., & Shankar, A. (2013). Purifying practices: How consumers assemble romantic experiences of nature. *Journal of Consumer Research, 39*(5), 1051–1069.

Carù, A., & Cova, B. (2003). Revisiting consumption experience: A more humble but complete view of the concept. *Marketing Theory, 3*(2), 267–286.

Carù, A., & Cova, B. (2006). How to facilitate immersion in a consumption experience: Appropriation operations and service elements. *Journal of Consumer Behaviour, 5*(1), 4–14.

Carù, A., & Cova, B. (2007). *Consuming experience.* New York, NY: Routledge.

Chambers, T. T., Price, L. L., & Jensen Schau, H. (2013). When differences unite: Resource dependence in heterogeneous consumption communities. *Journal of Consumer Research, 39*(5), 1010–1033.

Cova, B. (1997). Community and consumption: Towards a definition of the linking value of product or services. *European Journal of Marketing, 31*(3/4), 297–316.

Gourville, J. T., & Soman, D. (2005). Overchoice and assortment type: When and why variety backfires. *Marketing Science, 24*(3), 382–395.

Helkkula, A. (2011). Characterising the concept of service experience. *Journal of Service Management, 22*(3), 367–389.

Helkkula, A., & Kelleher, C. (2010). Circularity of customer service experience and customer perceived value. *Journal of Customer Behaviour, 9*(1), 37–53.

Holbrook, M. B., & Hirschman, E. C. (1982). The experiential aspects of consumption: Consumer fantasy, feelings and fun. *Journal of Consumer Research, 9*(2), 132–140.

Iyengar, S. S., & Lepper, M. R. (2000). When choice is demotivating: Can one desire too much of a good thing? *Journal Personality Social Psychology, 79*(6), 995–1006.

Lanier, C. D., & Rader, C. S. (2015). Consumption experience: An expanded view. *Marketing Theory, 15*(4), 1-22.

Latour, B. (2005). *Reassembling the social: An introduction to actor-network theory.* New York, NY: Oxford University Press.

Markman, A. B., & Medin, D. L. (1995). Similarity and alignment in choice. *Organizational Behavior Human Decision Processes, 63*(2), 117–130.

Martin, D. M., & Schouten, J. W. (2014). Consumption-driven market emergence. *Journal of Consumer Research, 40*(5), 855–870.

Muniz, A. M., & O'Guinn, T. C. (2001). Brand community. *Journal of Consumer Research, 27*(4), 412–432.

Pine, B. J., & Gilmore, J. H. (1999). *The experience economy: Work is theatre and every business is a stage.* Boston, MA: Harvard Business School Press.

Reckwitz, A. (2002). Towards a theory of social practice: A development in cultural theorizing. *European Journal of Social Theory, 5*(May), 243–262.

Tversky, A., & Shafir, E. (1992). Choice under conflict: The dynamics of deferred decision. *Psychological Science, 3*(6), 358–361.

Zhang, S., & Markman, A. B. (1998). Overcoming early entrant advantage: The role of alignable and nonalignable differences. *Journal of Marketing Research, 35*(November), 413–426.

CHAPTER V

Consumer Experiences of Choice Overload

Guilt, Turmoil and Emptiness

Hélène Cherrier and Lauren Gurrieri

5.1 Introduction

> In the mythic tradition, the Mountain is the bond between Earth and Sky. Its solitary summit reaches the sphere of eternity, and its base spreads out in manifold foothills into the world of mortals. It is the way by which man can raise himself to the divine and by which the divine can reveal itself to man.
>
> — René Daumal, Mount Analogue, 2004

Rene Daumal describes Mount Analogue as the ultimate sacred mountain. It connects the mortal to the divine, "uniting Earth and Heaven" (Daumal, 2004, p. 8). In consumer research, consumption is increasingly playing the sacred role of Mount Analogue. From the "Heaven on Earth" in Heritage Village, USA (O'Guinn & Belk, 1989), to the eternity of Apple Newton (Muniz & Schau, 2005), consumers experience material goods, consumption activities and brands as "magico-religious experiences" (Muniz & Schau, 2005, p. 746) to access the sacred (Belk, Wallendorf, & Sherry, 1989). In this enchanted mythical view, authors describe consumption as a religion (O'Guinn & Belk, 1989; Scott & MacLaran, 2009), a new faith (Miller, 1998), a transcendental vehicle (Belk, Wallendorf, & Sherry, 1989), and a magical and enchanting activity (Arnould, Price, & Otnes, 1999). As consumption "becomes a vehicle for experiencing the sacred" (Belk, Wallendorf, & Sherry, 1989, p. 1), an interplay arises between consumers' desires for enchantment and the responsiveness of commercial markets to provide objects and experiences that consumers can rework and refashion for this purpose (Thompson, 2006). In turn, consumers convert into spiritual followers (Simon, 1992), commodity exchanges are imbued with rituals and ceremonies (O'Guinn & Belk, 1989), brands become divine icons of worship (Muniz & Schau, 2005), and shopping centers transform into cathedrals of consumption to which we make "pilgrimages" to practice our consumer religion (Ritzer, 1999). Even the very term "religion" has been claimed by key consumer culture actors, with Delony Sledge from Coca-Cola professing, "our work is a religion," and John Lennon—the "God" of rock and roll—preaching that "we're more popular than Jesus" (Bronson, 1985).

Significant to our purpose is Rene Daumal's observation that previously sacrosanct mountains have lost their sacredness. Mount Everest, once unique and impossible to summit, has lost its sacredness as a result of intense commercialization (Daumal, 2004). Similarly, literature on excessive, over, or hyper-consumption contends that excess vulgarizes consumption to the point of dullness and disenchantment. Excess and its disenchantment have been discussed in studies on downshifting and minimalist lifestyles (Cherrier, 2008, 2009; Cherrier & Murray, 2007), de-growth movements (Cherrier, Szuba, & Ozcaglar-Toulouse, 2012), sustainable and responsible consumption (Kjellberg, 2008), and anti-consumerism (Dobscha, 1998). Similar to the Frankfurt School's concern with massification and the impact of commodification on social relations and the individual psyche, a central argument in these studies is that the spread of a consumerist/materialist market society—with its mass media and advertising, excessive commodification of life, falsification, simulations, and omnipresence—is disenchanting. For several decades, it has been observed that the increasing availability of positional goods lessens the value and benefits they offer (Hirsch, 1976), and that we live in a world of overabundance that renders material offerings and activities unexciting (Lipovetsky, 1987). This colonization of everyday life by commodification has come to provide an overwhelming array of symbolic meanings and cultural fields to choose from, problematizing the possibility for self-expression (Baudrillard, 1998). Rather than considering consumption as a sacred source of identification, lifestyle, and tastes, processes of massification and commodification have disenchanted the object-subject relationship, rendering it one characterized by despair (Baudrillard, 1998; Cherrier & Murray, 2007). In this disenchanted view, consuming beyond a certain point is entropic (Csikszentmihalyi, 2000; De Graaf, Wann, & Naylor, 2001), alienating (Borgmann, 2000; Fromm, 1979; Gergen, 1991; Holt, 2002), and stressful (Schor, 1998). The term "affluenza" equates consumption with a viral disease, spreading "a painful, contagious, socially transmitted condition of overload, debt, anxiety, and waste resulting from the dogged pursuit of more" (De Graaf, Wann, & Naylor, 2001, p. 2). Excess therefore does not enlighten, but rather drowns the consumer.

Our study explores how consumer disenchantment is experienced under conditions of excess driven by choice overload. First, we review Mount Analogue's loss of sacredness and relate Daumal's (2004) perspective to literatures on consumption. Second, we discuss three narratives that shed light on how disenchantment is experienced under conditions of choice overload—namely as guilt, turmoil and emptiness. Finally, we challenge the conceptualization of choice as rational and autonomous.

5.2 Mount Analogue and the Loss of Sacredness

Rene Daumal's depiction of Mount Analogue helps understand the fragility of sacredness and how sacred objects of consumption are rendered profane. To remain sacred, Mount Analogue's "summit must be inaccessible, but its base accessible to human beings.... It must be unique" (Daumal, 2004, p. 32). It is this inaccessibility by ordinary human beings that makes Mount Analogue a transcendental vehicle to the sacred. In parallel, for consumption to play the role of Mount Analogue, it must be perceived by all, but only accessible to a few who possess extraordinary means. The unique character of sacred consumption resonates with studies on commitment, love, allegiance, passion, devotion, involvement, and intimacy which support that emotional attachment occurs only with particular and a limited number of objects (Fournier 1998; Muniz & Schau, 2005). As Ahuvia notes, the vast array of objects and activities leads consumers to carefully select "only a handful" to love (Ahuvia, 2005, p. 182). Due to particular histories, features and emotional connections, these objects are appropriated and perceived as unique to their owner. This occurs through a process of singularization that involves consumers' successive meaning investments in an object and decommoditizing rituals that ensure certain objects of consumption remain unambiguously singular (Kopytoff, 1986).

Research on hyper-consumption confirms the fundamental role of perceived uniqueness in giving value to objects. As early as 1976, Hirsch noted that the increasing availability of positional goods vulgarizes consumption to the point of blurring its uniqueness. For Hirsch, consuming can only confer superiority and status if positional goods remain scarce. In a similar vein, Lipovetsky advances that we live in a world of excess that renders material offerings and activities so similar to one another that they become non-differentiable (Lipovetsky, 1987). This lack of differentiation vulgarizes acquisition and material possessions to the level of dullness. Following Hirsch and Lipovetsky, consuming in a world of overabundance and accessibility cannot be analogous to Mount Analogue, for it eradicates the uniqueness and inaccessibility of consuming.

For consumption to be a vehicle to sacredness, its access should be comparable to climbing Mount Analogue—it needs to be difficult and improbable to summit. This necessary difficult accessibility is explicit in Belk, Ger, and Askergaard's (2003) study on desire, where one informant states, "How can I desire what I can just go and buy" (p. 340). To exist, a desire needs to confront difficulties in reaching the object of desire. When desiring consumption inspires reverence and demands commitment and sacrifice, it is elevated to sacredness. Muniz and Schau's (2005) study supports clearly that extensive energy and ongoing efforts are required to reach sacredness (Belk, Wallendorf, & Sherry, 1989; Muniz & Schau, 2005). Yet, sacredness is never fully reached. As Rene Daumal (2004) writes, "You cannot always stay on the summits" (p. 105). To access the sacred, ongoing efforts are required relentlessly (Belk, Wallendorf, & Sherry, 1989).

Our review highlights that the growing abundance of consumption choices in a world of material excess makes it increasingly difficult for consumers to experience consumption as sacred. Instead, consumption often becomes disenchanting. Yet, how is consumer disenchantment experienced when choice becomes a problem as opposed to a freedom? The purpose of this chapter is to investigate this question.

5.3 Studying Consumer Disenchantment and Choice Overload

To investigate consumer disenchantment and choice overload, we analyzed interviews collected from individuals who participated in the broader project of simple living. In other words, these participants sought actively to consume less and more simply, as opposed to being overwhelmed and seduced by the vast number of choices available to them (Cherrier, 2008). Each informant was interviewed using phenomenological procedures that lasted between 90 and 260 minutes (Cherrier, 2005). The data analysis was directed initially by the question of what drives one to interrogate the value of consuming? What are the motivations, experiences, and emotions that lead to questioning the value of spending more and working more? Questioning involves experiences of discontinuity, differentiation, and fragmentation. How do consumers come to doubt the belief that consumption provides happiness? And in turn, how is this then experienced as disenchanting? For this study, we focused our queries on the role that the overload of consumption possibilities played in fostering this disenchantment. Below, we offer three narratives that illustrate our key findings, namely that disenchantment resulting from choice overload and excess is experienced as guilt, turmoil, and emptiness.

5.4 Research Findings

Three case studies exemplify how consumers experience choice overload as disenchanting, namely as experiences of guilt, turmoil and emptiness.

Case 1: Denise and the disenchantment of guilt

With an education in geography and political science, Denise, 25 years old, has read many articles and books relating to what Beck (1999) calls a "world risk society," learning about the deterioration of natural resources and the interconnectedness of the world. She understands the complexity of production, repartition, distribution, consumption, and waste, and its impact on the future of the planet. Her narrative offers a vision of an uncertain future. Confronted with the awareness of environmental degradation, Denise discusses how past generations have created a system that will destroy the natural ecosystem, and questions whether the rural environment of her childhood may disappear in the future.

> "I just became more aware of environmental problems. Getting older and reading and hearing about things, and environmental problems that have to do with consumption and workers in other countries and stuff like that. The more I became aware of the world and how things are connected and interrelated, it just became more and more obvious to me that the kind of consumptive lifestyle that everybody lives almost is just really bad for our future. I think the UN calls it 'intergenerational prejudice.'"

Being aware of living in an interconnected world brings a heavy burden to Denise's everyday consumption. She explains how she experiences great difficulties shopping and visiting retail stores. Her struggle is explicit when she describes the purchase of a 1600 square feet house with her boyfriend. While living in a big house, Denise experienced an increased drive to acquire and use a dizzying array of different products. Yet, instead of these choices bringing pleasure, they bred feelings of guilt for the potential environment degradation they harnessed. The material features of the house and its furniture arrangements entangled with Denise's environmental awareness, disturbing the seeming freedom of her consumption choices. For Denise, choice overload is equated with excessive consumption and waste.

> "When I bought the house, there were a whole lot more things that I needed to buy and to do that probably isn't good for the environment. So there was a lot more of those kinds of decisions that I had to make when I bought a house. Like I have to use - like when I took out the carpets, because there was an old wood floor underneath, and I wanted to finish it, and I had to use chemicals and lacquer and all that stuff. I used it. I'm not the best example of somebody who has this totally earth lifestyle. I have to buy stuff for the house, all kinds of stuff."

The environmental and moral significance of everyday consumption choices to maintain her house has become a burden for Denise. She describes an overwhelming guilt of being aware of the connection between her consumption and environmental degradation. The grand narrative of the environmental consequences of consuming provides a moral space for overpowering disenchantment.

> "There are so many things that contribute and perpetuate those lifestyles that it's really hard to see how it's going to change in a big way. Our whole economic system is based on consuming things that we don't need. And there's no stopping that."

Denise is not hopeful that changing her consumption behavior will assist in the protection and recovery of the natural environment. Moreover, she experiences ongoing guilt for the choices that she makes which contribute further to this degradation.

Case 2: Francois and the disenchantment of turmoil

Francois, a 27 year old man, lives in a clean house with his girlfriend and her daughter. As a child, Francois lived with his mother and brother in a place of chaos—"unorganized" and overcrowded with material objects. Growing up in a chaotic environment, Francois experienced anxiety and frustration. He could not understand why his mother surrounded them with unnecessary material possessions. He perceived that it made her life too complex and hard to manage. She was not happy and constantly wasted time searching for misplaced objects. For Francois, his mother suffered from a "saving disease," which enslaved her to material accumulation and misery.

> "I think it was watching the way that she lived her life and feeling like she was unhappy, she was burdened by these things. . . . And I guess I felt anxiety and didn't feel like her life was as good as it could be."

Francois' feelings of anxiety and frustration for material accumulation increased when his mother and father divorced and fought over their sons' affection using material gifts. At age 13, Francois perceived material possessions as a precursor to unhappiness, complexity, and emotional conflict.

> "My father was in a better economic situation than my mother, and my mother would go out of her way to get nice things for my brother and me, and if by chance my father had purchased the same thing for us she would be very upset and I have bad associations as far as giving material things as gifts."

Later in his teens, Francois realized he would not be happy living in a crowded environment like his mother. The abundant material choices that surrounded him were a source of chaos and difficulty for him that were profoundly not enjoyable. Instead, while visiting his father and grandmother, Francois discovered the positive emotional value of living in an organized, empty space, deprived of the overload of choices of unnecessary objects. On vacation at these houses, Francois did not experience the anxiety and unhappiness he felt at his mother's crowded place.

> "There was a contrast when I would visit my father and his wife is very different and was reasonably organized. And I didn't feel like he had the same anxiety, unhappiness, the same burden and so I guess at some point I made that connection. My mother's mother, we would visit her rarely. A couple of times a year, I guess. And her house was very - she lived there alone, but it had been a family residence and it was very large and empty. It was tidy. I was more comfortable there."

Though Francois has a clear desire for material simplicity, he nevertheless does not manage to live without the chaos of choice overload surrounding him. For example, Francois described moving to a dormitory for college at the age of 18, where he shared his room with an American boy concerned with fashion and electronic possessions. Confronted with his roommate's ongoing cycle of different material objects, Francois re-experienced the feelings of anxiety and frustration he felt while living at his mother's cluttered house. After graduating from university, Francois moved in with his girlfriend and her child, where once again he had to accept living surrounded by an array of material objects.

> "I get overwhelmed by these surroundings even though they're comparatively sparse to some people's environment."

Francois feels frustrated by the amount of objects that still surround him and yet, his narrative depicts an inescapability from the material—as experiences of consumption entangle him inevitably with other people. Yet for Francois, consumption and its concomitant choices breed turmoil—an anxiety and unease that are only remedied when the overwhelming variety of consumption choices around him are limited.

Case 3: Annie and the disenchantment of emptiness

Annie is a 25 year old woman deeply involved in Goth and punk sub-cultures. Annie lives in a three-bedroom apartment with a couple of rabbits, two huge dogs, three cats, a snake, and several rats. At 23, Annie divorced her husband, who left the relationship and marital home with half of their possessions. Annie found that she could not cope with the house's newly empty space and used consumption as a form of self-medication for her loneliness. Seduced by the choices that surrounded her, she re-acquired objects to feel "at home" again.

> "I was used to living with it so I thought I needed it. I was used to it around, so I went out and bit by bit re-acquired almost all the same stuff that I had had. Now we have the matched set again. Then bit by bit, I started to realize, especially it was an emotional thing. And in a way I was almost using like my friends did, the shopping as almost an emotional medication to make myself feel better. Well, I won't feel alone if I have enough furniture in the house. There's not this empty spot where the big easy chair used to be. Maybe I won't feel so abandoned."

Annie's narrative illustrates how despite being aware of the emotional crutch her possessions provide, she nevertheless surrenders herself to consumption to fill the void left by her husband. Similar to Denise, consumption is entangled with practices performed within the home; a home, she explains, that dictates her consumption and drives its disenchantment:

> "I live in a three-bedroom house. And that's another thing that I have to have stuff, furniture to feel up the space and stuff like that."

Consumption here becomes a necessity, even when undesired. Annie resembles a consumer trapped by an endless desire to fill up the void through the material and daily practices of consumption. The vast array of products that she consumes to fill her home is driven seldom by need, leaving her to ruminate and despair as to why she has purchased them to begin with: "I'm cleaning my cabinet and I am like 'blender? I own a blender! Why do I own a blender? I've never blended anything in my life.'" Annie believes that her urban lifestyle is responsible for her consumerist mentality. The dilemma of having so much to choose from does not bring pleasure or satisfaction, but rather a feeling of emptiness for the unnecessary and excessive consumption it stimulates:

> "The culture of the city really got to me and I kind of went overboard there in a way, even to excess. It's like you can go out to the club or the bar or dancing or the poetry reading or the play or the opera, because we do have opera come through here, or the orchestra or go to some event at the university, a lecture or seminar. Come here and do their store tour. And so you wind up dressing up a lot more . . . Which is why I think the whole clothing and fashion and the makeup and all the fun you can have with it really ensnared me. It's my big place where I go to excess, I know. Because the concept of clothes that aren't functional but are just fun was so new and interesting and entertaining."

For Annie, the short-term excitement that these possibilities bring is outweighed by their inevitable pointlessness. She laments on the enduring void consumption and accrued possessions bring to her life: "It doesn't matter all this, I am still alone". This exacerbates the futility of a consumption mentality driven by the pursuit of more and the endless search for the "right" item.

5.5 Discussion and Conclusion

Our chapter first discussed how the increasing proliferation of consumption choices has changed the landscape of consumption to one that is disenchanting. In this context, we investigated how consumers experience this disenchantment of choice overload as guilt, turmoil, and emptiness. Our findings also highlight that consumption choices are embedded in our social and cultural sphere and are not always made rationally. For example, past personal histories and relationships may color how the seemingly simple consumption choices and decisions involved in decorating one's home are enacted. Likewise, one's personal beliefs about the fragility of the environment may render what, on the surface, appears to be a pleasurable consumption act—such as seeing a film—a wasteful experience. As such, this chapter challenges the long-standing assumption that consumers make choices through an internal mental process that rationalizes the world around them. A number of authors have noted that consumption choices are rational, cognitive decisions linked to information-processing, awareness, and autonomy (see Allingham, 2002). By emphasizing these factors, it is inferred that consumers have the power to make informed decisions regardless of the context. This essentialist position conceptualizes consumers as rational individuals in control of their personal consumption choices. The control is exercised by the conscious mind on the body via free choice, autonomy, rational decision-making, self-regulation, and risk management. This perspective of empowered consumers making rational choices is appealing, but may not adequately consider a society fueled by an overabundance of consumption choices.

The notion of a rational and conscious individual has been disrupted in consumer culture theory studies, where consumption choices are often irrational, socially constructed, and culturally constrained (Arnould & Thompson, 2005). For example, if we consider a post-structural perspective on consumption choices, consumers are not independent individuals free to make rational decisions. Rather, they are influenced by a system of codification, symbolic representations, and social norms. Here, consumption practices are not the consequence of a rational decision-making process existing independently of social and cultural discourses. On the contrary, the post-structuralist view positions consumption choices as both constrained and enabled by cultural and social discourses which, in turn, take part in constructing these discourses (Shankar, Cherrier, & Canniford, 2006). Accordingly, our knowledge on what, when, how much, with who, and where to consume is socially and culturally enabled and constrained. By revealing the tensions and conflicts that underlie choice overload—namely experiences of guilt, turmoil, and emptiness—this chapter challenges the conceptualization of choice overload as operating in a rational vacuum.

5.6 References

Ahuvia, A. C. (2005). Beyond the extended self: Loved objects and consumers' identity narratives. *Journal of Consumer Research, 32*(1), 171–184.

Allingham, M. (2002). *Choice theory: A very short introduction.* Oxford, England: Oxford University Press.

Arnould, E. J., Price, L. L., & Otnes, C. (1999). Making magic consumption: A study of white water river rafting. *Journal of Contemporary Ethnography, 28*(1), 33–68.

Arnould, E. J., & Thompson, C. J. (2005). Consumer Culture Theory (CCT): Twenty years of research. *Journal of Consumer Research, 31*(4), 868–873.

Baudrillard, J. (1998). *The consumer society: Myths and structures.* London, England: Sage Publications.

Beck, U. (1999). *World risk society.* Cambridge, England: Polity Press.

Belk, R. W., Ger, G., & Askegaard, S. (2003). The fire of desire: A multisited inquiry into consumer passion. *Journal of Consumer Research, 30*(3), 326–342.

Belk, R. W., Wallendorf, M., & Sherry, J. F. (1989). The sacred and the profane in consumer research: Theodicy on the odyssey. *Journal of Consumer Research, 16*(June), 1–38.

Borgmann, A. (2000). The moral complexion of consumption. *Journal of Consumer Research, 26*(4), 418–422.

Bronson, F. (1985). *The billboard book of number one hits.* New York, NY: Billboard Publications.

Cherrier, H. (2005). Using existential-phenomenological interviewing to explore meanings of consumption. In R. Harrison, T. Newholm, & D. Shaw (Eds.), *The ethical consumer* (pp. 125-136). London, England: Sage Publications.

Cherrier, H. (2008). Understanding the process of becoming a downshifter: An orienting conceptual framework. In F. Gandolfi & H. Cherrier (Eds.), *Downshifting: A theoretical and practical approach to living a simplified life* (pp. 22-48). Hyderabad, India: The ICFAI University Press.

Cherrier, H. (2009). Disposal and simple living: Exploring the circulation of goods and the development of sacred consumption. *Journal of Consumer Behavior, 8*(6), 327–339.

Cherrier, H., & Murray, J. B. (2007). Reflexive dispossession and the self: Constructing a processual theory of identity. *Consumption, Markets & Culture, 10*(1), 1–30.

Cherrier, H., Szuba, M., & Ozcaglar-Toulouse, N. (2012). Barriers to downward carbon emission: Exploring sustainable consumption in face of the glass floor. *Journal of Marketing Management, 28*(3/4), 397–419.

Csikszentmihalyi, M. (2000). The costs and benefits of consuming. *Journal of Consumer Research, 27*(2), 267–272.

Daumal, R. (2004). *Mount analogue: A tale of non-Euclidian and symbolically authentic mountaineering adventures.* Woodstock, NY: Overlook Press.

De Graaf, J., Wann, D., & Naylor, T. H. (2001). *Affluenza: The all-consuming epidemic.* San Francisco, CA: Berrett-Koehler.

Dobscha, S. (1998). The lived experience of consumer rebellion against marketing. In J. W. Alba & W. Hutchinson (Eds.), *Advances in Consumer Research* (Vol. 25, pp. 91–97). Provo, UT: Association for Consumer Research.

Fournier, S. (1998). Consumers and their brands: Developing relationship theory in consumer research. *Journal of Consumer Research, 24*(2), 343–373.

Fromm, E. (1979). *To have or to be?* London, England: Abacus.

Gergen, K. J. (1991). *The saturated self: Dilemmas of identity in contemporary life.* New York, NY: Basic Books.

Hirsch, F. (1976). *Social limits to growth.* Cambridge, MA: Harvard University Press.

Holt, D. B. (2002). Why do brands cause trouble? A dialectical theory of consumer culture and branding. *Journal of Consumer Research, 29*(June), 70–90.

Kjellberg, H. (2008). Market practices and overconsumption. *Consumption, Markets and Culture, 11*(2), 151–167.

Kopytoff, I. (1986). The cultural biography of things: Commoditization as process. In A. Appadurai (Ed.), *The social life of things* (pp. 64–94). Cambridge, England: Cambridge University Press.

Lipovetsky, G. (1987). *L'Empire de l'éphémère : la mode et son destin dans les sociétés modernes* [*The empire of fashion: Dressing modern democracy*]. Paris, France: Gallimard.

Miller, D. (1998). *A theory of shopping.* Ithaca, NY: Cornell University Press.

Muniz, A. M., & Schau, H. J. (2005). Religiosity in the abandonned Apple Newton brand community. *Journal of Consumer Research, 31*(March), 737–747.

O'Guinn, T. C., & Belk, R. W. (1989). Heaven on earth: Consumption at heritage village, USA. *Journal of Consumer Research, 16*(2), 227–238.

Ritzer, G. (1999). *Enchanting a disenchanted world: Revolutionizing the means of consumption.* Thousand Oaks, CA: Pine Forge Press.

Schor, J. (1998). *The overspent American: Upscaling, downshifting and the new consumer.* New York, NY: Basic Books.

Scott, L., & MacLaran, P. (2009). 'Roll your own' - religion: Consumer culture and the spiritual vernacular. In A. L. McGill & S. Shavitt (Eds.), *Advances in Consumer Research* (Vol. 36, pp. 60-63). Duluth, MN: Association for Consumer Research.

Shankar, A., Cherrier, H., & Canniford, R. (2006). Consumer empowerment: A Foucauldian interpretation [Special issue]. *European Journal of Marketing, 40*(9/10), 1013–1030.

Simon, R. K. (1992). The formal garden in the age of consumer culture: A reading of the 20th century shopping mall. In F. Wayne & M. Steiner (Eds.), *Mapping American culture* (pp. 231–250). Iowa City, IA: University of Iowa Press.

Thompson, C. J. (2006). The McDonaldization of enchantment and consumers practices of reenchantment: A dialectic view of transformative consumption. In C. Pechman & L. Price (Eds.), *Advances in Consumer Research* (Vol. 33, pp. 352–354). Duluth, MN: Association of Consumer Research.

CHAPTER VI

Inane Questions and Unquestioned Lies in a Postmodern Age of Overchoice

Erin O'Neill-Armendarez

6.1 Authenticity

In a recent article published online (Pattuglia, Mingione, & Cherubini, 2015), researchers concluded that consumers are searching for authenticity from brands. This quest has become especially important as overchoice and disillusionment appear to have left consumers hungry for a company they can trust. Consequently, the establishment of brand authenticity, whether for a product, company, or political campaign, has, according to Brown, Kozinets, and Sherry (2003), become "one of the 'cornerstones of contemporary marketing'" (p. 21). The article goes on to affirm that, "a company can be seen as authentic if there is consistency between espoused values, ideal identity, and how it actually behaves" (Pattuglia, Mingione, & Cherubini, 2015, p. 5).

What is a company to do? Apparently, it has become necessary in the current climate for vigorous, repetitive marketing research to supply data to corporations proving to them the profitability of telling the truth living up to their claims.

The article goes on to coach interested marketers on how to establish trust with consumers, as if honesty were some mysterious commodity difficult to acquire. Unfortunately, in the current climate, perhaps it is. Why would this be important? According to the authors, "it should be noted that authenticity not only leads to consumers' trust, but also to consumers' willingness to pay a premium price" (Pattuglia, Mingione, & Cherubini, 2015, p. 4).

The upshot of this research, analysis, and argument in an age of overchoice is that companies should attempt to seem trustworthy in order to achieve their highest goal: to make more money. They can achieve this best by "aligning" corporate behavior and practice with brand claims. At the risk of sounding naïve, one might ask, shouldn't that be obvious? Apparently it is not, and several readily available case studies underscore the point painfully.

Americans are called "consumers" more often than we are called citizens—it is apparently our civic duty to consume liberally in order to avoid economic recession—and many of us were raised to trust certain sets of democratic values, one of which is the freedom to make choices in the pursuit of happiness. We have been taught to believe that democracy will usually, if not always, produce the most creative solutions to problems and the most meaningful lives for most members of our society. In addition, many Americans have been taught to depend upon the Judeo-Christian values that informed the "founding fathers"—although this claim has rightfully been challenged—along with Benjamin Franklin/Horatio Alger-type initiative and self-reliance. If we work hard, if we are honest, if we are optimistic and work and play well with other hard-working, decent people, we will live good lives and advance ourselves individually and as a society. During the industrial and modern periods of Western history, it was commonly believed that Science (with a capital S) and reason would win the day, preventing or solving all or most of the problems of human civilizations, disease, and the most serious effects of natural disasters like drought, hurricanes, and even aging. Many of us had likewise been taught, via a somewhat distorted version of Adam Smith's "invisible hand" argument, that individuals and companies could produce the most prosperity for all by focusing solely on how to prosper themselves. Everyone, many have assumed, is capable of becoming a millionaire with a bit of initiative. This is just one of the myths of capitalism, one of the United States' grand narratives, and it is all too obvious that many Americans still believe it. They are tuned into Powerball lottery winner announcements on the news, or game shows where smart, lucky contestants are given the chance to become millionaires if they can just make the right choices quickly. They have to hurry—there is not much time before the next spate of commercial advertisements.

From the time they are able to sit up in their high chairs, many American children are exposed to an onslaught of confusing, divergent messages—those which are terrifying (police shootings) next to those that excite (Pop-Tarts!)—and our nation has done relatively little to protect these growing minds, preferring all too often to defend corporate freedom of speech instead. In this postmodern third and last phase of capitalism, it is an end game: money trumps everything. Consumers are free to choose from a staggering, ever-growing mountain of choices, but they are unlikely to ever have the opportunity to understand the true consequences of many of those choices. A privileged few are able to bombard consumers with sophisticated messages that influence and even create their worldviews before those individuals ever have the opportunity to learn how these messages govern their thought and behavior, making it increasingly difficult for them to determine what is healthy for them to feed their children, which products are actually safe, and which candidates are most likely to legislate and vote toward their interests. Dark money can pay for an unlimited number of sensationalized, ad hominem campaign messages to destroy the chances of a candidate unable to secure a large enough war chest. Even though the Supreme Court has ruled on the legality of gay marriage, a county clerk in Kentucky is still a hero to many for refusing to issue marriage licenses to same-sex couples. After all, it is against her religion, and it is always right to uphold one's religious values, even when one is apparently confused about whether one's religion should govern one's own moral decision making, or that of the rest of the world. When the clerk is jailed for contempt of court, the clerk's pitiful case seems much stronger, as oversimplified either/or thinking replaces deep reflection on the constitutional separation of church and state and how that protects all citizens equally under the law, including the clerk.

Learning to understand and solve ill-structured social and economic problems is expensive. One must be fortunate enough to have access to high-quality education. In addition, one must have the time and will to sort through the varying claims, facts, hidden biases, and motives attached to the avalanche of conflicting messages. Those unable or unwilling to contemplate all the information available on the legality of gay marriage or the shooting of Michael Brown in Ferguson prefer simply to pick a side and an accompanying slogan. It is much more difficult to reflect upon a possible solution to the plight of Syrian refugees attempting to escape—many with infants and small children—the horrors of ISIS (Islamic State in Iraq and Syria). The moral challenges posed by their suffering are certainly more problematic than the either/or choice offered viewers in reference to the Kentucky clerk's attempt to avoid the fires of hell: should the clerk, or shouldn't the clerk? Viewers are encouraged to weigh in—they either believe the clerk should issue those licenses, or that the clerk should not.

That is all the major networks have time for before they play the required commercial messages ad nauseam, subsequently returning to their divergent stream of bytes and images: a chicken holding up traffic on a bridge near Oakland, a video clip of the scatter-brained fowl running under, between, and around cars in heavily-jammed morning traffic, the news anchor laughing as a woman in the video says, "just let it run." From there, the anchor segues quickly to a female college student from Virginia hanging from "Murder Wall"—a 6,000 foot high vertical limestone rock face in the Alps—then to a shot of John Kerry recovering from his bicycle accident after tense negotiations to halt the possible development of an Iranian nuclear weapon, and then to the president giving stern warnings about global warming from Alaska after he had signed recent legislation allowing for oil drilling in the Arctic. A visitor from another time or place, past or future, might be likely to conclude after witnessing this inexplicable, incoherent barrage of inanity that we must all be insane. Such a visitor would find it impossible to make sense of such a conflicting parade of messages—the urgent juxtaposed with the ridiculous. Logically speaking, those who support the Kentucky clerk should also uphold the rights of vegetarian servers to refuse to serve steak at Applebee's or Chili's. Of course, those servers would be fired instantly, and the only ones to support their refusal would be People for the Ethical Treatment of Animals (PETA) and the Humane Society. When reason and reflective capabilities are trumped by the packaged storylines that replace the ability to make sensible comparisons or to listen to reason, then it is just one set of platitudes hollering at another. No one is heard, and the best choices of all, the best solutions, never even make it to the table for careful consideration.

A recent study attempts to prove that drinking Coca-Cola does not cause obesity directly (O'Connor, 2015); another has discovered that eating fast food actually is as good for professional athletes as drinking Gatorade (Cramer et al., 2015), which may actually be true, since 20 ounces of the sports drink may contain 35—and sometimes even 41—grams of sugar (Pirotin, Becker, & Crawford,

2014, p. 17), leading Berkeley researchers to conclude that it may be contributing to obesity in children. Gatorade contains enough sodium to increase the risk of high blood pressure among those who consume the beverage regularly. Obviously, the average person would be better off consuming neither fast food nor Gatorade; comparing the two as a post-workout meal for athletes seems consequently absurd. Nonetheless, searching "fast food and Gatorade" on the web provides a long list of sources announcing the merits of fast food for professional athletes.

One of the identified challenges of postmodern thinking—the embracing of all the various truths, all the voices, all the diverging experience—is the apparent implication that all messages are equally valid. If one speaker is invited to appear on a news program to discuss an issue, another who is diametrically opposed must also be invited. They will have dueling sets of facts, and the one who interrupts the other the most, or is loudest and most aggressive, is often perceived to be the most right. Viewers, unless they are able to sort through the intimidating pile of available "facts" and anecdotal evidence available online and in print, and are also able to recognize bias and expertise, will never be able to ascertain which source portrays an incident or issue most accurately. In addition, those viewers are less and less likely to have the time, assuming they are literate and have access to this information. Authenticity is not the only rare, precious commodity in this brave new world—time, energy, and attention seem equally rare. Hence, Donald Trump seems completely comfortable insulting journalists openly for asking him "tricky" questions, finding it more important to prove that his hair is "real" than to provide polite, detailed answers in order to establish himself as a viable candidate for the highest office in the land. Voters are attracted to him because he seems real. They like his no-nonsense statement from his TV show *The Apprentice*—"You're fired"—and believe, apparently, that this is the approach for solving the problems of the day. It does not seem to matter that Trump's leadership style might prove disastrous in handling delicate negotiations where insulting the opponent would be ineffective at best and cataclysmic at worst. Viewers seem to have conflated the fictional world of reality TV with a Super Bowl-type hype that is becoming the milieu of American politics. If Trump has signed a promise not to run as a third party candidate, it is not legally binding, the newscaster explains, and so it goes. The most pressing needs of the day are buried under a ridiculous pastiche of insults and insignificant factoids meant to distract consumers toward advertisements and away from serious reflection on problems like global warming, the shortage of water in California, and the war in Syria.

At the same time, American popular media, movies, and television programs continue to reify our most common grand narratives—those plots where the Americans always overcome the evil Russians (or Muslim terrorists, or alien invaders, or vampires, or zombies). Scientists always save us from intermittent apocalypse, starving entrepreneurs replace temporary homelessness with untold wealth simply by following their dreams, and the hero who does what is Right wins in the end, defeating his or her opponent inevitably. Many Americans are still invested highly in these myths, which to some degree distract them successfully from readily available alternative truths and the ambiguities of the more postmodern polyglot of voices, groups, and causes. All these are attempting to establish trust with beleaguered consumers, citizens faced with an exponentially growing number of difficult choices to make in a society where technology, while it has undoubtedly made some things easier and better, has also caused us all to have to adjust to an increasingly confusing onslaught of messages delivered via smart phones, tablets, laptops, and Cable TV or Internet entertainment providers, whether we want them or not. Such consumers, too tired or frightened to contemplate the alternatives, can simply select the pre-packaged stories of their choice—those that comfort them as lullabies calm a restless infant.

6.2 Postmodernism

In his 2002 re-posting of an article entitled "The Implications of Postmodernism for Psychotherapy," Blatner, MD, notes that the disadvantages of living in a postmodern society can overwhelm an individual psychologically. He notes the subjectivism and relativism that naturally evolve in a postmodern culture, acknowledging that, "in its extreme form, this philosophy denies the objective and subjects all truth to the filters of experience," (Blatner, 2002, p.1) replacing absolute truth with constructed truths. He points to Adler's assertion that "constructs in the mind"—also commonly referred to as "schemas" or "fictions"—are the best we can do in our attempts to conceptualize, interpret, and understand a fast-paced, complicated world. Small wonder so many prefer the oversimplified escape offered by the grand narratives of science, religion, and politics, even if upon closer examination they often turn out to be oversimplified assumptions touted as absolutes.

Blatner points out that while the average citizen is unaware of postmodernism as an intellectual movement, its relativistic effects stemming from the plethora of voices and claims, each holding its own truth, is a sort of de-centering of identity for those individuals who no longer have complete confidence in the grand narratives, yet are paralyzed by the ensuing ambiguity.

He advises psychotherapists to help each troubled individual to shift from ambivalence and confusion to creativity and social interest—to assist each in constructing his or her own "personal mythology" (Blatner, 2002, p.3). The gnawing question remains: Why should they? Why should it matter? If no absolute can be trusted, then what is the point of attempting to individuate successfully anyhow? Might not one be just as satisfied acquiring as much material wealth as possible? Isn't that the message repeated over and over and over again in an age where the acquisition of wealth appears to be more important than character? If the bumper sticker slogan "He who dies with the most toys wins" seems arrogant and foolish, one had better turn quickly to "Jesus Saves," or "Might Makes Right," or the equivalent before anxiety, stress, and/or depression become overwhelming, as they already have for many Americans. In spite of the successes of psychotherapists in helping patients overcome the oppressive list of possibilities from which to select their beliefs and behaviors, many consumers are becoming desensitized to the repeated exposés and video portrayals of movie stars, preachers, politicians, murderers, and random citizens offering justifications for their violent, criminal, or anti-social behavior. Such repetition may cause aberrant behavior to seem much more mainstream than in actuality, as dueling lawyers or journalists offer varying alternatives to explain why someone might enter a movie theater and shoot dozens of random strangers. Could there ever be a logical reason for such behavior? Postmodern theory tells us it is a matter of perspective, and reasoning minds must acknowledge this horrific truth: it *is*. Faced with the possibility that lasting truth cannot be grasped, many lapse into a useless, fatalistic cynicism, ignorant denial, or chronic anxiety or depression.

Blatner offers some useful strategies for dealing with the fragmentation of identity caused by the replacement of absolute truth with an uncomfortable relativism. However, these strategies are only likely to work in individuals and communities that are, as he points out, able to reflect and acquire metacognitive skills (Blatner,

2002, p. 5) that will allow them to unpack their own assumptions, their own biases and fears, and the interference of their own negative emotions. In the past, and for some in the present, the unwavering belief in a pre-packaged set of core values and social norms adopted by family, friends, and community made the development of metacognitive abilities unnecessary for many. People believed what they believed, and often did their best to avoid open difference of opinion—they did not discuss sex, religion, or politics at public functions or parties, and everyone seemed to get along just fine. The deconstruction of grand narratives has, for many people, revealed the moral harm of such thinking and behavior. But the dissolution of one set of assumptions is an easier feat than the development of another. For untrained minds overwhelmed by too much information and too little time, the successful acquisition of more useful norms and truths—particularly when these minds are increasingly distracted by more and more media messages—becomes less and less likely. Sure, marketers may be able to fool them into trusting a company brand and paying more for something. But we may (is there a "we"?) have more important things to worry about.

Instead of careful reflection and consideration of Buber's other, consumers of popular media are inundated by repetitious, oversimplified claims that they are urged to accept without question. What good would it do to question anyhow? Machiavelli already addressed that problem centuries ago, establishing that only the rare few dare question the prevailing claims of the powerful. In a society where the enlightenment belief in the value of reason appears to be somewhat passé, it is unarguably easier to adopt the assumptions du jour of one's immediate circle, or those simultaneously offered by all three major networks' morning news programs (CBS, NBC, and ABC) than to wonder, is this true? Does it matter? What good would it do the viewer to know? Thus, many are convinced that Kim Kardashian's wedding vows may have been less than sincere, that soccer is a game more of us should be watching, and that England's royal family is worthy of continued, relentless scrutiny. When the most recent Bachelorette confessed in the last moments of the season, just as Bachelor A was about to get down on one knee, that she had finally realized Bachelor B was her soul mate, devoted viewers expressed their satisfaction or regret on Twitter—their postings were almost instantaneously displayed on the screen for audience consideration, and millions were entertained. Was it really Love? It did not matter. Either way, it was fun, right? There were snap moral judgments, and an engaging spectacle to voyeuristically view as the expensive diamond (should not we all be sporting those?) was pulled from Bachelor B's pocket for the admiration of all. The difference between cheering for a football team or a fictitious (real?) TV character or a candidate for president is lost for many, who are content to absorb snippets of oversimplified rhetoric on the gun control debate in the wake of the Sandy Hook shootings. Somehow, any meaningful discussion of alternatives for treating serious mental illness (not an excuse, of course, but certainly a relevant topic) cannot get much air time, perhaps because there is no time for the complexity, or we have all concluded there is no money for implementing solutions anyhow. As for gun law reform in the United States, we are repeatedly assured that the National Rifle Association (NRA) is too powerful, case closed.

What is the societal impact of the growing lack of logic in the explanations attempting to justify the actions of those at the helm of our most trusted institutions—our schools, our local, state, and federal governments, our churches, and our hospitals and doctors—as our young receive more and more information on scandal, lawsuit, and inefficiency? Is trust possible? Our football heroes and priests turn out to be pedophiles, as do some of our teachers. We cannot escape the married politician who is involved romantically with a high-end prostitute making way more money than the average worker will ever earn, or the likewise married senator who sends photos of his genitals to a teenager he met online. Is it possible to ascertain a useful truth in such a cultural milieu, other than "God is great, beer is good, and people are crazy"? We will not be able to build much of a future on that, unfortunately, in spite of the recent proliferation of truly excellent craft beer nationwide.

Our gifted youth—particularly females—are in many cases overwhelmed by their career choices, often unsure of what to "do" with themselves, even when they are grounded enough to have a sense of what they would like to do (e.g., make money, make the world a better place, or achieve fame or glory). There are so many possibilities and there is so much pressure. The idea that they should simply pursue a rewarding career, marry a dependable guy and have kids is off the table; finding that perfect college, the right career choice, or the dependable guy—"the one"—has become so much more difficult, and studies show that the focus in mating seems to have shifted from finding someone compatible to finding the "best" possible partner from an Internet or speed dating catalog of thousands. Many still believe in soul mates, but how can a person be sure that *this* one is that person? Apparently, this is a complicated question, as the heroines of soap operas and romantic comedies are usually infuriated and repulsed by their True Loves until the last twenty minutes or so of the movie or series. Recently, the television show *Mistresses* has offered for entertainment the emotional angst of a psychotherapist who first dated her client and then became involved sexually with a married couple, moving into their house and receiving her own key, which for her signified something of deep importance. The apparent message to viewers of all ages? It is possible for a successful psychotherapist to enter into a deeply committed sexual relationship with two people at the same time, and these people might be married to each other and of different genders, both quite content to share. This is just one of the many narratives played out in serial episodes over the nation's airwaves, potentially entertaining for viewers with fairly stable identities, values, and beliefs, but quite likely to confuse impressionable young viewers trying to understand their bodies, the possibility of lifelong monogamy, and the prospect of raising children in a world where today's truth becomes tomorrow's "mistake." Each story of deviance, each horrific corpse displayed in shocking detail (it's okay, they're not real) introduces viewers to another perspective, another way of being or acting. Why shouldn't viewers who see stories just as shocking headlining the evening news or their favorite web page begin to believe we are a nation of deviants in sore need of the right medications?

While marketers are doing their best to reach the right niche markets, each of which is involved in its own version of reality, consumers are often underprepared to contemplate the actual differences between "virtual" and face-to-face identities and interactions, and more and more research tells us they are relying on the opinions of their peers to decide who to trust and what to purchase. Given the choice between expert product reviews involving elaborate product testing and the anecdotal opinions of people who seem like themselves, many consumers prefer the more straight-forward blurbs written by a handful of random strangers, along with the photos they post to confirm the validity of their claims. In the current climate, brands cannot maintain consumer trust or credibility without a healthy list of customer endorsements, so companies now solicit opinions via email. Responses are automatically tabulated, compiled, and sorted so that opinions about a product or service can be made available instantly to anyone wishing for information on the quality of almost any product. Everyone's opinion seems equally valid.

6.3 Information Overchoice and Misinformation

In their 2009 article "The Dark Side of Information," Bawden and Robinson discuss the anxieties and pathologies that information overload poses, which they assert are not necessarily new phenomena, but are becoming more prevalent as people attempt to find useful information available in the Web 2.0 environment, which includes "a variety of sites and tools for shared information creation and updating, and social networking and communication" (p. 7). In this environment, they point out, it becomes exceptionally difficult to determine source authority and expert qualifications, allowing trusting consumers to be deliberately or unwittingly misled by pseudo-experts. The nature of information promoted by Web 2.0 is "based on *shallow novelty* [italics from Bawden and Robinson]" and leads to "an expectation of constant novelty," as opposed to a valuing of a slower, more careful compilation of reliable facts (Bawden & Robinson, 2009, p. 7). Because it is more difficult to generate new information, the Web 2.0 environment favors a quick re-packaging of old material into "soundbites" and "microchunks" which cannot offer consumers the actual complexity or depth necessary for authentic understanding. As sustained attention has become more difficult to achieve, and appears to have limited value for all but those trained to analyze the consequences of facile, fragmented human cognition, most consumers would probably not be willing or able to invest the time or energy required for exploring fully all aspects of a complex problem, or even all the competing claims surrounding a candidate for whom they might vote.

In an environment where there is information "push," even highly educated researchers find it impossible to keep up with all the email, and all the new journals and websites offering new information on important subjects of interest. These researchers may have to deal with the phenomena Billig (2013) outlines bravely in *Learn to Write Badly: How to Succeed in the Social Sciences*. Instead of accurate and transparent reporting of the results of findings, they may encounter journals filled with overblown, pseudo-scientific claims of ambitious academics more interested in establishing a career than in advancing human knowledge in an authentic, meaningful way. While some may respond to information overload by simply avoiding information, others have learned a strategy known as "satisficing" (Schwartz, et al., 2002)—limiting the amount of information consumed to include just enough to meet the immediate information need at hand. While the consumer may be aware that there is more, possibly even better information yet to be reviewed, he or she opts to make a decision once satisfied that enough information has been explored. So long as the decision or product generated from "satisfying" meets the goal, it is deemed good enough. The possibility of a better decision or product is abandoned because the consumer realizes there is simply not enough time to absorb it all. Bawden and Robinson (2009) emphasize the importance of reason in satisficing. Without careful reasoning, consumers opting for satisficing may end up with results that will not meet intended needs.

While career professionals and trained academics will most often be able to apply reason effectively while satisficing—although they may experience significant anxiety while attempting to do so—American citizens with short attention spans and time constraints will be unlikely to meet the required standard of reasoning for effective satisficing in their attempts to use information in their own better interest. In her book *Distracted: The Erosion of Attention and the Coming Dark Age*, Jackson (2008) echoes this concern, citing several studies that confirm the shrinking ability of the average citizen to focus on a single task, and the negative impact this has on a person's ability to successfully complete an important task or to reason carefully to make a crucial decision. Young minds are particularly at risk, as they have not yet had the opportunity to learn to control their cognitive processes or to develop stable identities before they are seduced into a virtual world of sights, sounds, and images—everything from television to video games to online pornography. Often, young people are not able to resist, and are unaware that their development into adulthood could be seriously compromised as a result. Unfortunately, they may be very vulnerable to sexual predators, bullies, or online communities aimed at converting confused, susceptible minds to oversimplified, violent extremism. Or, they may stumble upon ISIS—the "most successful terrorist brand ever"—whose social media campaigns make use of "Hollywood techniques, and branding strategies more commonly associated with the corporate world" (Petroff, 2015, p. 1). Like Trump, ISIS markets themselves as winners. According to J.M. Berger (2015), co-author of *ISIS: The State of Terror*, "from a marketing perspective, what they're selling is the image of strength" (Petroff, 2015, p. 1). He goes on to point out that ISIS has "advanced the art of storytelling," (Petroff, 2015, p. 2) creating documentaries with "Hollywood-esque cinematography" to capture the imaginations of potential recruits. Their slogan—"Enduring and Expanding"—along with their other marketing strategies, has attracted devotees seeking to be "part of something larger than themselves" (as cited in Petroff, 2015, p. 2).

Around 2010, the Defense Advanced Research Projects Agency (DARPA) invited top researchers at universities in the US to explore "the role narratives play in human psychology and sociology," (Defense Advanced Research Projects Agency, para. 1) announcing that such research may have "strategic implications for defense missions" (Defense Advanced Research Projects Agency, para. 1). According to the DARPA summary of related research projects, "narratives may consolidate memory, shape emotions, cue heuristics and biases in judgment, and influence group distinctions" (Defense Advanced Research Projects Agency, n.d., para. 3). DARPA recognizes that religious values can short circuit human reasoning (Gordon, n.d.). Instead of calling for research on how best to produce effective reasoning, reflection, and metacognition in minds susceptible to the appealing, oversimplified narratives offered by religious extremists, DARPA is apparently more interested in learning how to use the power of narrative to influence human cognition and behavior. As narrative is known to be the most ancient, most powerful tool for making sense of experience available to the human mind, to the point where it appears to be hard-wired into our DNA, DARPA's call for research invokes concern that the postmodern mistrust of truth and reason—which may at least be partially responsible for the anxiety and confusion of many adolescents and young adults attempting to develop identities among the smashed ideals lying in the rubble of Western grand narratives—may be deliberately replaced with well-crafted narratives. These narratives are crafted by a global oligarchy attempting to create a brave new world of sheeple who simply plug their experiences into the readily available templates to derive meaning or judgement, as opposed to carefully compiling facts and considering the impact of actions on varying stakeholders before deciding on the best course of action.

Arizona State University's Center for Strategic Communication received over six million dollars to "study the neurobiology of narrative comprehension, validate narrative theories and explore the connection between narrative and persuasion" (Arizona State University as cited in Swann, 2013). The money is being used to create video narratives meant to "control the thought process of groups of people. And ultimately to be able to trigger narratives through magnetic stimulation" (Swann, 2013). According to an interview with a supposed whistleblower who leaked the ominous nature of the actual research being done, the project aims to map the neural networks of master narratives to use "transcranial magnetic stimulation" to "turn off" narrative networking in the brain to bypass it with propaganda DARPA would use to "force people to accept the view of the U.S. that we desire them to have" (as cited in Swann 2013). In short, mind control.

While this experimentation is underway, the whistleblower challenges the notion that DARPA would only use such a strategy on "extremists":

> See, the problem with the question is who gets to define extremist? Who decides if religious beliefs are inherently dangerous? And if we believe that government should have the power to control how the extremist thinks . . . wouldn't they have the authority to decide how and what we all think?"(as cited in Swann, 2013)

The full proof of this mad science initiative is currently unavailable, as the leaked document belongs to Arizona State University, and they have chosen not to release it. An article on Wired.com raises the same possibility, describing the DARPA research aims thus: "tools will be used to detect who's been controlled by subversive ideologies, better allowing the military to drown out that message and win people onto their side" (Lim, 2011, p. 2). The article ends by warning, "forget lie detectors; invisible propaganda-detectors are the future" (Lim, 2011, p. 2). Another article's byline announces, "Pentagon researching 'narrative networks' as a way to hijack the brain with false stories" (Heyes, 2012). The article begins by asking, "If someone—or some government entity—were able to figure out the science behind what makes people violent, what do you suppose they would do with that knowledge?" (Heyes, 2012, para. 1). Citing a BBC report, the article claims that the DARPA Narrative Networks initiative ultimately means to "hijack the mind so it can implant false, but believable stories—a sort of 'like me' weapon, if you will" (Heyes, 2012, para. 2).

The article acknowledges scientific consensus on the power of narrative in human cognition, noting its "powerful sway over the human mind, shaping a person's notion of groups and identities and even motivating them to commit violence" (Heyes, 2012, para. 6). University of Colorado social psychologist Tom Pyszczynski doubts such a strategy could ever work. In order to keep people from resorting to extremist violence, he is convinced that "we're going to need to change the way they interpret things that happen and we're going to need to stop doing things that people interpret as insulting or challenging to their way of life" (as cited in Heyes, 2012, para. 11).

Whether the US government is in fact attempting to elevate the art of propaganda to a science, media dependency theorists claim an effective venue for influencing untrained minds is already in existence. Media dependence theory hypothesizes that the way news is "framed" has a powerful influence on audience. Entman's definition (1993) explains that news stories are often presented, or framed, "to promote a particular problem definition, causal interpretation, moral evaluation, and/or treatment recommendation" (as cited in Reese, 2001, p. 4). The media are "producing news as a commodity, generating frames that may distort as much as they illuminate our social world" (as cited in Reese , 2001, p. 19). Communication theorists have established that audiences look to various media outlets during times of instability. Therefore, these outlets have unusually powerful influence during unstable times, since consumers are trusting them to select and deliver the right information to help them form opinions and decide how to act (Stuart, 2014). Moreover, theorists agree that, "broadcast news is neither neutral nor objective, but interpretive" (Stuart, 2014, p. 6). As audiences become dependent upon media during times of difficulty, often seeing the same soundbites repeated over and over again on several news networks—the same faces, the same words, narratives with heroes, villains, and an often oversimplified portrayal of both—it is quite likely that most consumers will accept these interpretations of events as "fact," never bothering to wonder about which details have been excluded, or what else might be happening that was not covered at all.

Unfortunately, consumers with limited amounts of time and a decreasing ability to achieve sustained focus are very unlikely to pursue missing information on their own. Even if they made the attempt, as some do, these consumers would immediately encounter false information saturating the web deliberately, as we have seen in the case of global warming, for example. Only an information-literate consumer with resources, time, and sustained interest would be able to sort through the hundreds of thousands to millions of online sources all claiming expert knowledge on the subject at hand to find the best information offered by unbiased, current experts. How would they be able to recognize true experts among the burgeoning lists of companies, organizations, and institutes all offering them information on world events, political parties and candidates, and health-related issues? To evaluate all the free, available information on diet alone would probably take months—if not years—and since most consumers are unaware of the dynamic between the United States Department of Agriculture and organizations like the National Cattlemen's Beef Association, the National Dairy Council, and the Soft Drink Association, they will never be able to understand something as basic as the food pyramid, how it is constructed, and why it has been revised several times over the past few decades. In order to understand the dynamic, they would need to be highly literate as well as information literate. They would also have to be effective critical thinkers, able to shelve their own biases in order to understand the issues related to food production and the information released by the US government with respect to nutrition and human health. More than likely, consumers will be enticed by the first web page offering lists of scannable bullets and engaging pictures of appealing food. They will trust this page almost instantaneously without even bothering to determine who is offering them this information, and what might motivate content providers to create such a page. They will not notice that the descriptions of disease symptoms and causes they have researched were provided by pharmaceutical companies hoping to convince them that their drugs are a perfect remedy. Given that our society has reached the point where political action committees and special interest groups with power and money have the most influence on key institutions like health care and education—which have become for-profit organizations achieving record profits annually—it seems foolish to hope that politicians elected in such a climate would have the will to invest in education that would equip American minds to deal with the growing number of false, obsolete, or unreliable messages attempting to sell them something potentially harmful.

6.4 Educating

We have long known how best to encourage independent, critical thought. In spite of this, and in spite of all the billions of dollars spent on (and pocketed) in the pursuit of excellence in education, the US education system is, at best, an inexplicable failure in educating high school and even college students to evaluate information carefully and to think critically. Somehow, the elite have continued access to quality education, yet the apparently irresolvable social and cultural problems of our nation have left a disturbing number of K-12 students and adults either illiterate or functionally illiterate. As a result, these individuals and their progeny are especially vulnerable to the bombardment of sophisticated messages deliberately intended to influence choices detrimental to their own well-being, and are likely to adopt oversimplified beliefs, values, and philosophies that will not allow them to participate in productive civic conversation or to leverage power toward their own advantage in the workplace. Current rhetoric on education seems focused mainly on expensive standardized tests and "competing in a global economy." We are worried our students will not be able to do math, will not be able to "compete." We seem less worried that they will not be able to understand the implications of math application, how it changes their lives and alters their planet forever. We want them to think about conserving water, yet morning newscasts covering how most of our water is consumed, or addressing how most of our food is produced, are reduced to simple sound bites. It is obvious that bourgeois American consumers, who are educated and comfortable, have little interest in ferreting out exactly where steak or eggs come from, preferring to be shocked momentarily by the appearance of "pink sludge" as they drink their morning coffee and the subsequent disappearance of the topic forever from the news and from their minds. These consumers are too busy remembering dozens of passwords, answering email, logging onto their online bank accounts, catching up with their hundreds of friends on Facebook, and consuming the news and entertainment media. This busyness allows consumers to avoid the uncomfortable complexities of ill-structured problems like bridges in disrepair or weapons of mass destruction that actually were never there.

Meanwhile, next door (or in the next room), there is a teenager lost in the shuffle—a kid whose parents are doing the best they can, speeding back and forth between work, school, ball games, and church—or worse yet, addicted to prescription drugs or porn. This kid is looking for meaning in life, a chance to be recognized, and a plan for his life in which he will have power, can be a hero, and can exercise agency instead of being the passive recipient of competing messages from school and work about who he should be and why, and what he ought to do. These messages do not satisfy because they are oversimplified and lack an understanding of where he is and what is churning in his mind—a mind with no anchor, a heart without empathy, as he has so seldom seen actual empathy, except for in those stories on TV where dogs are rescued from swirling arroyos. His parents have given him a room, a TV, a cell phone, video games, the freedom to pursue what he wants in his free time, so long as he stays out of trouble, but they do not have time to sit with him, to gaze at him from across the dining room table, nor do they have the antidote for the powerful glut of social media and entertainment. What he could use is an ongoing series of frank conversations on how to find himself in this ocean of blurbs and images, a conversation on what he should trust in this world, and who, and why, a conversation about negotiating the incredible messiness of American culture. A pat on the back and a couple of slogans will not be a big enough Band-Aid for his growing confusion and his inability to relax or to concentrate. He might get lucky. "He'll be okay," his parents assure themselves. "It's normal. We went through it." No, they didn't. They have no idea. Sure, he might find a little niche group, do okay in school, find a way to make a living and to shut out the looming larger questions in favor of a nice car, a loving wife, or whatever else he decides will bring him happiness. Or, he might not.

If he is lower-middle class or is living in poverty, his chances of achieving anything positive at all are significantly diminished. He may be practically forced to join a gang in middle school so he can walk safely in his neighborhood, and his fellow gang members will not teach him to reason. They will teach him to obey without question, to do what he is told, to keep the truth silent, and to understand that gang leaders are just doing what the government is doing. They are just doing what the cigarette and alcohol companies are doing, what BP and Exxon and Monsanto are doing, what the world is doing: making money, and justifying their crimes—intentional or otherwise—by any means necessary. Some either/or thinker has probably decided his female counterpart should not have convenient access to condoms or birth control—the domain of the home, they say, as if that were logical given the current statistics—replacing an understanding of an incredibly complex problem with a tired platitude that somehow comforts them (a platitude attached to a narrative that replaces curiosity or the desire for deeper understanding). Maybe DARPA is wasting their money trying to replace choice with propaganda. Maybe that feat has already been accomplished, and most of us are just blissfully unaware.

6.5 References

Bawden, D., & Robinson, L. (2009). The dark side of information overload, anxiety, and other paradoxes and pathologies. *Journal of Information Science, 35*(2), 180–191. doi:10.1177/0165551508095781

Billig, M. (2013). *Learn to write badly: How to succeed in the social sciences.* Cambridge, England: Cambridge University Press.

Blatner, A. (2002). The implications of postmodern psychotherapy. *Individual Psychology, 53*(4), 476–482. Retrieved from http://www.blatner.com/adam/level2/pmodpsy198.htm

Brown, S., Kozinets, R. V., & Sherry Jr., J. F. (2003). Teaching old brands new tricks: Retro branding and the revival of brand meaning. *Journal of Marketing, 67*(3), 19-33.

Cramer, M., Dumke, C., Hailes, W., Cuddy, J., & Ruby, B. (2015). Post-exercise glycogen recovery and exercise performance is not significantly different between fast food and sport supplements. *International Journal of Sport Nutrition and Exercise Metabolism, 25*(5), 448–455. doi:10.1123.ijsnem.2014-0230

Defense Advanced Research Projects Agency (n.d.). *Narrative networks.* U.S. Department of Defense. Retrieved from http://www.darpa.mil/program/narrative-networks

Gordon, A. S. (n.d.). *Project: Neurobiology of narrative framing.* University of Southern California Institute for Creative Technologies. Narrative Group. Retrieved from http://narrative.ict.usc.edu/neurobiology-of-narrative-framing.html

Heyes, J. D. (2012, May 15). Pentagon researching 'narrative networks' as way to hijack the brain with false stories. Natural Health News and Scientific Discoveries. *Natural News.* Retrieved from http://www.naturalnews.com/035872_Pentagon_narrative_networks_propaganda.html

Jackson, M. (2008). *Distracted: The erosion of attention and the coming dark age.* Amherst, NY: Prometheus Books.

Lim, D. (2011, October 18). DARPA wants to master the science of propaganda. Danger Room. *Wired.* Retrieved from https://www.wired.com/2011/10/darpa-science-propaganda/

O'Connor, A. (2015, August 9). Coca-Cola funds scientists who shift blame for obesity away from bad diets [Web log post]. *New York Times.* Retrieved from http://well.blogs.nytimes.com/2015/08/09/coca-cola-funds-scientists-who-shift-blame-for-obesity-away-from-bad-diets/?_r=1

Pattuglia, S., Mingione, M., & Cherubini, S. (2015). Achieving alignment for corporate brand success: The consumer quest for authenticity and heritage. In J.C. Andreani & U. Collesei (Eds.), *Proceedings of the International Marketing Trends Conference 2015 Paris.* Paris-Venice Marketing Trends Association. Retrieved from http://www.marketing-trends-congress.com/archives/2015/pages/PDF/029.pdf

Petroff, A. (2015, May 7). ISIS: The most successful terrorist brand ever? *CNN Money*. Retrieved from http://www.money.cnn.com/2015/05/07/Media/isis-brand-media-twitter

Pirotin, S., Becker, C., & Crawford, P. B. (2014, August). *Looking beyond the marketing claims of new beverages: Health risks of consumer sports drinks, energy drinks, fortified waters and other flavored beverages.* Atkins Center for Weight and Health, College of Natural Resources, School of Public Health, University of California at Berkeley. Retrieved from http://healthyeatingresearch.org/research/looking-beyond-the-marketing-claims-of-new-beverages-health-risks-of-consuming-sports-drinks-energy-drinks-fortified-waters-and-other-flavored-beverages/

Reese, S. D. (2001). Framing public life: A bridging model for media research. In G. Reese & A. Grant (Eds.), *Framing public life: Perspectives on media and our understanding of the social world* (pp. 7–31). Mahwah, NJ: Lawrence Erlbaum.

Schwartz, B., Ward, A., Monterosso, J., Lyubomirsky, S. White, K., & Lehman, D.R. (2002). Maximizing versus satisficing: Happiness is a matter of choice. *Journal of Personality and Social Psychology, 83*(5), 1178–1197.

Stuart, B. (2014). From Selma, Alabama, to Derry, Northern Ireland: Media images and their influence on civil rights demonstrations. *Journal of Mass Communication and Journalism, 4*(6). doi:10.4172/2165-7192.1000200

Swann, B. (2013, October 16). Exclusive: Government program to control religious thought? [Video]. *Truth in Media.* Retrieved from http://www.truthinmedia.com/government-program-to-control-religious-thought/

CHAPTER VII

Tales of Ignorance and Greed

Toward Improving Social Mythology and More Conscious Choice

Erin O'Neill-Armendarez

7.1 Filtering Information to Make Better Choices

In a postmodern society where the grand narratives for many have been destroyed—or have, for others, been reified as oversimplifications in a complicated world—it is still possible for individuals to develop genuinely democratic values from which to make responsible choices under the right circumstances. It is possible for us as citizens to use Schwartz's "satisficing" (Schwartz et al. 2002) to arrive at decisions that will solve problems and allow individuals to select and eliminate options from an almost infinite number of choices in our personal and civic lives. However, it is increasingly unlikely that children and adolescents—whether they be living in poverty or in relative wealth—will be able to develop the necessary tools for filtering through piles of deliberately deceptive claims in order to develop democratic values from which to make effective choices. While parents, schools, and churches may expect kids to just do what they are told—and amazingly, some do—it seems obvious that many are not satisfied with oversimplified, either/or explanations of democratic, capitalistic, or Christian values that do not capture fully the realities of their lives. Many attempt to discover better explanations for things as they are, and, if they are not to regress to groupthink or to extremism—which for many seems to be the antidote to postmodern uncertainty and to the worn seams of oversimplified American and Christian ideals—they will need the right sort of upbringing and education.

A truly democratic society should embrace tolerance, diversity, and freedom of religion. The desire for a reactionary return to a nostalgic past is not only impossible, but it raises the very important question: how did we get here from there? It seems fairly obvious that the homogenous, peaceful past of ubiquitous wealth, harmony, and peace never actually existed in the US, as an honest review of our nation's history should make painfully clear. If the grand narratives of Western civilization were at their roots hegemonic, it was inevitable that one day these roots would be exposed as partial lies by marginalized and excluded populations. Likewise, the absurdity and fragmentation of extreme postmodern philosophy do not offer individuals useful guidelines for creating meaning in life from which to generate conscious, ethical choice. Practical strategies for managing information overload and for considering carefully the consequences of potential choices must be taught and reinforced if we are to improve the ability of the average American citizen to self-determine successfully and to participate fully in democratic decision-making on issues of grave importance like global warming and national security. If we are to provide high quality education, establish a sustainable economy, and increase opportunities for prosperity for all citizens rather than a few, we must give citizens the necessary tools for negotiating the fragmented, polyglot nature of the current milieu—which includes very sophisticated propaganda and marketing science meant to exploit the fears and desires of the masses.

From their earliest years in the American education system, students must be taught effective alternatives to either/or thinking. They must be taught to be aware of the strong pull of groupthink, as proven by a number of highly celebrated experiments. If we value critical questioning of untested assumption, if we value the ability to listen with attention and respect to viewpoints different from our own, then we should model these qualities and give students repeated opportunities to practice them until the behavior seems natural and most appropriate. Unfortunately, there are too few opportunities for students to witness polite, reasoned conversations in which speakers sort through a series of complex issues, explain their positions, and acknowledge truths in opposing viewpoints. Students must learn that the best choices emerge only rarely from automatic thinking that overrides unexamined motive.

The abilities to question one's own assumptions and to listen openly with delayed judgment are necessary for healthy individuals attempting to derive meaning from life in a democratic, postmodern society. According to psychotherapist Adam Blatner (2002), many individuals feel decentered in a society where "the sense of common consensus" (p. 1) which surely had been a comforting illusion—no longer exists. If reality is constructed, and there is no actual truth with a capital T, then what could be the purpose of an individual life, or of a nation, or of the world? When science, American democracy, religion, and celebrated heroes are flawed, and when social roles are no longer clearly defined, a type of nihilism seems a tempting choice. Yet Blatner poses a more hopeful alternative: the idea that individuals can be enlisted in the effort to construct a better reality absent of absolutes. Blatner (2002) suggests that social interest might replace individual narcissism and allow individuals to see others as essential in constructing that better reality. Instead of digging trenches in defense of absolutes, people would develop "a willingness to consider new information in the light of the present moment" (Blatner, 2002, p. 3). Although such an approach may have features of existentialism, it is a healthy alternative to nihilism. It recognizes the constructed nature of human reality, and it offers a profound opportunity to take responsibility for our beliefs, values, assumptions and subsequent choices, even in the face of uncertainty.

According to Blatner (2002), individuals must learn to give up the "illusion of 'being right'" and the preoccupation with winning in order to approach problems from "radically new and different points of view" (p. 3). Without the hegemony of the grand narrative, the individual is liberated to generate his or her own sense of purpose, and to respect the creative and personal choices of others. Individuals can focus on "a personal religious journey" and can enjoy sharing that journey with others who hold similar values, so long as groups do not become rigid and elitist in their thinking. Blatner (2002) draws a synthetic conclusion from the work of Adler, Jung, and Rank: "People do have some degree of intuition regarding their connectedness with the greater wholeness of things" (p. 4). Blatner mentions Viktor Frankl's ideas on the human search for meaning, which appears to exist in us all. That search becomes distorted—or even evil—when one individual's quest for truth threatens others. When only one choice is believed socially or morally acceptable in a given situation, the dehumanization and even demonizing of those who refuse that choice is the inevitable result.

Blatner points out that within individuals are many "sub-selves." Those able to recognize and reflect upon these selves understand more easily their own impulses and motivations. When conscious reflection on these impulses and motivations is repressed, individuals whose identities depend upon the delusion of superiority—those engaged in an endless quest "to be or have more, to do better" (Blatner, 2002, p. 4)—are subject to exploitation by marketers and propagandists with a highly sophisticated knowledge of human psychology. Thus, according to Blatner, psychotherapists should encourage their patients to learn to respect other worldviews and to develop metacognitive skills. Further, he insists that self-awareness, interpersonal problem solving, and communications should become foundational to twenty first-century curricula, as they will teach individuals essential skills, habits, and attitudes for the onslaught of potentially confusing issues they may face—everything from gender neutral restrooms to legal euthanasia. People without these skills will become quickly polarized, automatically building defensive walls that will shut out alternative voices quickly, and hoping to dominate and eventually destroy other points of view or ways of being.

Blatner (2002) places particular emphasis on the ability to shift point of view, and to analyze carefully and reflect upon the varying perspectives and assumptions related to a particular issue or problem. He is confident this ability can be taught and is "the needed next step in the evolution of consciousness" (Blatner, 2002, p. 6). While the flaws and problems inherent in the grand narratives of Western culture have been exposed, it does not logically follow that humans should give up attempting to create a better world or to find meaning in life. Perhaps it means that somehow we need to own our choices, to take responsibility for their consequences, and to more fully understand the multiple parts of ourselves which—under the right circumstances—might revert to less rational, less effective ways of deciding. When a society develops a shared set of values, those values are refined and improved continually. If the best representations of truth are understood as those grounded in dialectic, then it will be less possible for individuals or communities to exclude or to dominate others, either inadvertently or deliberately. The refusal to engage in respectful, open dialogue is the choice of dictators—those uninterested in achieving harmonious, pluralistic societies. The mindless reaction of the angry mob—the inability to articulate a position, the inability to listen or to effectively negotiate a mutually acceptable solution—is likewise an automatic choice.

7.2 Using Rogerian Analysis to Find Choice Solutions

Rogerian analysis is a fairly well known strategy for teaching students to consider the priorities of the multiple—possibly polarized—groups of stakeholders wrangling over a complex problem. Instead of reifying positions that are already rigid, Rogerian analysis attempts to establish common ground among stakeholders. Here, choice again involves some degree of metacognition and an awareness of the concerns of others. Rogerian analysis acknowledges that all stakeholders may have valid, even pressing, concerns. Rather than attempting to drown out those concerns, or to ignore them, or to justify one's own concerns as more valid or more "right," a Rogerian analyst attempts to establish a solution that respects the views of all and meets the most needs possible. There is no absolutism in Rogerian theory. Acknowledging the concerns of others, as opposed to diminishing them, offers rich reward and encourages mutual respect and trust. While individual freedom is an American ideal, that freedom is often not considered through the lens of public responsibility. Many people seem to believe that they have the freedom to do whatever they choose, not understanding the impacts of their choices on others, on the environment, or even on their own families. Something as simple as the choice of whether or not to wear a motorcycle helmet becomes much more complex when the concerns of all possible stakeholders are first recognized and then carefully considered. The individual still retains the power to choose, but the choice becomes more than an indicator of a personal preference or a refusal to bow to the will of others. It becomes an acknowledgement of our interconnectedness and our interdependence. If children and adolescents were taught to value choices made in this sort of way, they would become less likely to believe propaganda that excludes or devalues those who are different. They might even develop the ability to consider the impacts of all of their consumer choices, political choices, and relationship choices beyond themselves, taking into account the impact of their decisions on all involved stakeholders.

The evolution of the human brain and its thinking processes involved the evolution of the ability to make split-second life-and-death choices, often without any conscious thought. An animal that stops to consider the impact of its choices on all stakeholders in the wild might fall prey to a hungry predator before a decision could be made. Thus, it seems the human brain is actually more comfortable reverting to instinct than it is negotiating conflicting, complex, and interconnected details related to a single problem. Delaying a choice or a decision sometimes has serious consequence. While the most primitive thought sequence in the brain appears to be very crude narrative (first this, then that), the brain stores possibilities in terms of simple binaries—often polar opposites. It is easy in a story to sort the hero from the villain, and the brain has a natural tendency to sort and classify quickly for survival. The brain recognizes black or white instantly, but has no interest in identifying all the different shades of white, black, and gray available for contemplation. Fortunately, our higher order thinking capabilities, as well as our empathy and imagination, allow us to temporarily shelve hasty conclusions and existing assumptions in order to shift perspectives, to see subtlety, and to use metacognition to gain a deeper understanding of the complexities of a problem. We can do it, but we have to have the time to do it. We also have to see the benefits to ourselves, as well as to others, that such thinking will provide. In short, we have to *want* to use our higher order thinking capabilities to do more than prove ourselves "right." At the same time, we must accept that a deeper consideration of the facts and consequences related to any particular choice may not initially bring satisfaction, but may cause further confusion, possibly frustration, and ultimately disappointment.

Hence, a parent responds to the persistent questioning of a child with "do it because I said so!" This logic makes no sense, but it solves an immediate problem. However, it is likely to create a larger problem later when the child, lacking the reasoning beyond the choice, will not be able to apply it in his or her own better interest. Similarly, a political candidate can distract viewers during a debate by making fun of an opponent's appearance, and a disturbing number of viewers might think that's funny. They share the candidate's latent sense of superiority over the unlucky person being ridiculed. Somewhere in the back of their minds they know this is against our democratic values fundamentally, but it takes effort to reflect on this, and a deeper reflection might lead viewers to confusion when it comes to deciding how to vote. There are any number of choices a person can make that do not require much reason—which football team to root for, what color to paint the kitchen, etc.—where personal preference does not require any sort of careful deliberation. Certainly, there are people predisposed to careful analysis in any sort of decision making, but those people are undoubtedly in the minority. Still, most of us go to the supermarket under the assumption that all the products are safe, and that there are regulations in place to protect us from serious harm. Looking more carefully involves an inevitable uncertainty once we realize that even with the best of intentions, people make mistakes. We are trusting others with important details of our lives every day. We assume the plane we board is in good repair and that the Transportation Security Administration (TSA) staff have prevented anything harmful from being brought onto the plane. Without these basic assumptions, we would become paralyzed—unable to move or act. We assume there is a very low probability that on any given day one of our assumptions will prove incorrect. However, the law of probability necessitates that at some point, at least one of our assumptions (the theater is safe, the packaged lettuce is safe) will indeed turn out to be false, possibly ushering in disaster. Knowing this, we rely still on our assumptions in order to move about the world and to go about our business.

7.3 Avoiding Choice Paralysis

How, then, do we decide any particular assumption, oversimplification, or overgeneralization deserves additional time, energy, and attention for more careful analysis and reflection? Time, energy, and attention are less and less available in our frenetic work weeks, and fewer and fewer of us pause to contemplate seriously the statements of a celebrity-turned-politician, or the root causes of serious social, environmental, or economic problems that do not seem to have immediate impact on our lives.

Most voters do not know how their favorite candidate's campaign is funded. They know very little about where their food comes from, or how it is made. They are unaware of the primary cause of water shortages, or why health care continues to become exponentially more expensive every year. This lack of awareness does not mean that these voters are not capable of knowing this information. Rather, the lack of awareness indicates that voters do not perceive a need to know the information, and so do not realize how non-biased facts and opinions from experts might enhance their ability to make better choices. Some voters may be repressing a silent fear of some hidden, unpleasant truth that they do not feel equipped to handle. What if they find out that the chickens they eat are raised inhumanely, or that the slaughterhouse workers are pressured to adopt an unsustainable pace of production? What then? It is not true that what you do not know cannot hurt you; still, we all have the impulse to close our eyes and hide in the corner when the monster appears. Certain sorts of choices, even some of the most mundane—e.g., where you buy your shoes—might become dangerously complicated if a few more facts were thrown into the mix. A sort of paralysis, a pleasant self-distraction (in this culture, it has never been easier) takes away the fear of the monster. If the monster is going to get you anyhow, why bother fighting?

Could this be the reason so many in the twenty-first century appear to prefer alcohol, marijuana, and opiates to authentic civic engagement? Blatner's (2002) vision for a collaboratively constructed society built on creativity, flexibility, and mutual respect can only be possible if people have the time, attention, and courage to develop the capabilities necessary to fight the overgeneralization, oversimplification, and mindless repetition of the same reductive facts that have no apparent use—the ones that distract us away from our own ambivalence, doubt, and fear. This is the territory we must traverse in order to be able to make fully informed choices, recognizing that our uninformed, automatic choices may cause harm to ourselves or others. What would propel us to devote the time and energy to make such discoveries? Isn't it easier just to tell ourselves that we have built the greatest nation in the world? That we deserve whatever we want? That whoever does not like us is inherently evil in some way?

Individuals and societies can and do move toward more equitable, more harmonious and sustainable choices, but most of the members of our society are more interested in a good boxing match than in an extended, reasoned debate on any topic, even one as serious as shifting weather patterns or species extinctions. Consequently, any debate had better involve a fairly short, bulleted list. There had better be a clear, concise summary for the busy executives and legislators. Otherwise, they would not take the time to read it.

It seems easiest to fall back on standard assumptions and narratives than to consider the disturbing alternatives. Are we as Americans who we think we are? Are we "the greatest nation on earth," the moral beacon of the globe—as our politicians repeatedly claim—or are we the only nation on earth to have ever detonated an atomic bomb? Is it possible we are a bloodthirsty, imperialistic nation whose citizens feel an unquestioned entitlement to everything on the planet simply because we believe we are better? Or are we a nation of deluded "consumers," deliberately distracting ourselves away from our lack of certainty in ourselves and in each other? Which narrative contains the best, most accurate picture of who we are? Or, is that a matter of perspective, depending on experience? Unfortunately, many of us are not able or willing to consider alternate possibilities against the comfort of our oversimplified assumptions. How do we make conscious, informed choices without first developing the ability to shift perspectives on how our world came to be as it is and on our own role in perpetuating that world? The more attention we pay, the more energy we expend. The more awake we are, the more we know, and the more difficult it becomes to make the choices we may want to make, or own our true reasons, or air our actual motivations and deliberations in front of everyone. A tweet is much safer than a reason, even if it is offhand and unfortunate. It is easy to just say, "oops, I had a bad day," than it is to say, "yes, that is my deliberate conclusion. Does it displease you?"

In *Learning to Write Badly,* Billig (2013) argues courageously against the unnecessary proliferation of research, which he says is mass-produced across all disciplines. Billig (2013) faults the business model for the exponential increase in scholarly productivity, where researchers are producing more and more "knowledge" in the wake of ever increasing competition (p. 19). According to Billig (2013), 2,900 new articles a week are published in the social sciences alone (p. 27). It would be impossible, he argues, for any scholar to read everything published in his or her discipline. The mass marketing of scholarly work has caused academics to read like non-academics, and it has become more and more common for academics to consume media by niche as opposed to looking for connections beyond their own immediate interests. Scholars must confine their specializations to smaller and smaller fields of knowledge simply because there is too much to read and to know when that area is broadened (Billig, 2013, p. 29). The obscurity, and in some cases "meaninglessness," of some published articles was underscored when Alan Sokal published a deliberate parody of postmodern theory in a scholarly journal (Billig, 2013, p. 3).

If well-trained, information-literate academics are struggling to make meaning in their fragmented, shrinking disciplines, it should come as no surprise that American consumers—particularly teens and young adults—often lack the tools, time, and motivation required to filter information in order to make the best choices on what to buy, for whom to vote, and how best to preserve their health and that of their children and aging parents. In spite of the wealth of knowledge provided on cognitive development and on the workings of the human mind, our educational system in some ways appears to have side-stepped the obvious difficulties involved in solving ill-structured problems—whether personal or civic—in the presence of so much false and misleading information. For example, well-intentioned students, parents, and teachers may spend an inordinate amount of time discussing improvements to our educational system, but how many of them are aware of the well-documented conflicts of interest between the edupreneurial quest for public money and the civic responsibilities of elected and appointed officials? Americans faced with the possibility of diseases like rheumatoid arthritis, diabetes, irritable bowel syndrome, and Alzheimer's disease are bombarded with sophisticated advertisements created by marketers well aware of the impact of these repeated messages on the untrained human mind. However, these same Americans are ill-equipped to search out the relationships between diet and these diseases. If they do seek such information, they encounter oversimplified solutions provided by pharmaceutical companies and the for-profit medical industry that have driven a disturbing number of US citizens into bankruptcy. When deciding what to purchase, consumers hoping to learn how their food, clothing, or personal care products are produced will encounter piles of competing claims from companies, product reviewers, and watchdog organizations on issues like animal cruelty, the safety of additives, and the working conditions of those who produce these goods. It would take days to read through all the information on the suits and countersuits involving the accusations against large companies. Consumers need the information literacy skills necessary for recognizing field-specific expertise and hidden bias. The stakes have never been higher.

7.4 Good Enough: Accepting Things as They Are

Chernus (n.d.), in his article "Frederic Jameson's Interpretation of Postmodernism," argues that the desire for "wholeness" creates a solvable problem for the postmodern citizen: "When the pieces of our experience don't fit together, we naturally feel disappointed and deprived. . . .The truth is that pieces of world and self never fit together. So once we forget about seeking unity and totality we are ready to face reality and live honestly" (p. 1). To accept things as they are, a person has to *want* to come to this realization; he or she needs not only the time, but also the right sort of social and cultural environment to wade into uncertainty. Otherwise, as Chernus (n.d.) points out, people will be tempted to lapse into belief in a master narrative that could be quite harmful. How is this possible in a postmodern world? It is easy, because in spite of scientific discovery, the postmodern landscape is dotted with simulacra that "cut us off from the real past and future, because they give us such comfortable substitutes" (Chernus, n.d., p. 8). As a result, "fundamentalists also fit in very well with postmodernism" (Chernus, n.d., p. 18).

Fundamentalists use the media very effectively and can conjure the key elements of their grand narrative easily with a carefully worded sentence or two—which is all they have time for in the typical sound bite anyhow. For the individual unwilling to accept a less certain, less predictable world, such a narrative must have strong appeal. If Jesus supposedly said, "those who live by the sword die by the sword," or "violence begets violence," if he never bothered to try to raise up an army against the Romans (although ostensibly he was God, capable of anything, including walking on water and raising the dead), these inconvenient truths do not seem to worry the typical religious fundamentalist, whose grand narrative of apocalypse and Christian supremacy into the afterlife and beyond has been completely co-opted by radio talk show hosts, celebrity pastors and their television broadcasts, and the lucrative publication of books, magazines, and music meant to help individuals avoid actual thought about the disturbing photos of drowned Muslim children washing up on the shores of Greece. See, they are Muslims—so—that word gets plugged in, and the rest might quickly be God's judgment, inevitable. If he has no mercy for these children, why should we? The humanity of others is silenced by the insistence that we all *must* worship Jesus. If we do not, we'll have bigger problems than drowning in the Mediterranean, right? This mentality exhibits either/or thinking at its most frustrating, yet its persistence as undeniable propaganda defies rational human thought, not to mention core Christian values like nonviolence, love and empathy. If an apocalypse is all we can hope for, we are ironically sharing the dream of ISIS, and we are all in trouble.

Cognitive narratologists from previous decades offer some useful approaches to the baffling and somewhat disappointing refusal of many American citizens to recognize the ethical consequences of their unwillingness to carefully analyze and reflect upon the automatic assumptions that govern their choices. In "The Narrative Construction of Reality," Bruner (1991) explains that narrative—the human mind's most primitive and prevalent construct for making meaning—is mostly concerned with "verisimilitude," but not "empirical verification." Thus, the brand narrative that satisfies the consumer's quest for authenticity only needs to *seem* credible (Bruner, 1991, p. 4). To verify a brand or company's values or ideals would be practically impossible. What matters, then, is what *seems*. Marketers know this; those who market politicians know it as well. But citizens and consumers all too often do not have the metacognitive tools to reflect usefully upon their own either/or thinking, or to recognize it as a basic human tendency that can hurt us if we have not learned to use our higher order thinking capabilities, or if for whatever reason (we are busy, we are afraid, we are angry, or all of the above) we are not willing.

Bruner uses the example of Orson Welles' *The War of the Worlds* broadcast to illustrate how narrative can trick or seduce. Consumers are subject to "narrative banalization," which desensitizes them to the point where they no longer attempt to interpret actively the parts of a story, or to reconsider alternative interpretations (Burner, 1991, p. 9). While narrative has the power to cause viewers, listeners, or readers to rethink unchallenged assumptions, it also has the power to reinforce false assumption, and is exploited shamelessly by marketers who delude consumers unapologetically and deliberately. Let the buyer beware, but what if the buyer is unable to unpack the narrative, having internalized its heroes, villains, and happy endings since infancy? McDonald's well knows the value of imprinting toddler minds with the Golden Arches; the parents of the child, much less so. In this case, narrative is used to usher in the end game, where consumer and citizen choice involves nothing more than moving in accordance with the groupthink of the narrative. Movies, advertisements, and mass media all assure us that these choices are the best choices. To question these claims takes curiosity, information literacy skills, persistence, courage, and sometimes empathy—all qualities of a successful critical thinker that should be encouraged and modeled for youth. In his groundbreaking book *The Literary Mind,* Turner (1996) says of narrative, "we rarely notice these stories themselves or the way they work because they are always present" (p. 12). The cognitive processes involved in internalizing stories are not always available for conscious reflection, unless we become attuned to the elements of story and how they function. Jerome Bruner and Ira Chernus seem to agree that humans cling to narrative as an alternative to solipsism. We create the sense of a shared experience through the lens of narrative. For these reasons, citizens in a democratic society must understand how narratives forge values—moral constructs that merge reason with emotion.

7.5 Deciphering the Choice Code

For millennia, human beings have used narrative to teach cultural values to their children. In a civilization where the narratives of capitalism still veil the counter narratives of exclusion and poverty, a novel like Richard Wright's *Native Son,* or a nonfiction narrative like Dave Eggers' *Zeitoun* may prompt readers to think more carefully about learned assumptions; unfortunately, for every citizen reading such a book, there are dozens immersed completely in crime drama and the oversimplified ethnic stereotypes the entertainment industry offers. Narratives that question the values of capitalism or fundamentalism represent a small stream against the ocean of advertisement and deliberate propaganda oversimplifying the reasons for poverty in America or for war in Iraq, Afghanistan, and Syria.

Frye's (1972) short missive *On Teaching Literature* is considered dated by many literary scholars. Nevertheless, it seems Frye may have been ahead of his time in recognizing the dual nature of narrative. He recognized that societies use narrative, or what he called "adjustment narrative," to create social mythology and cultural ideology (Frye, 1972, p. 16). He identifies two aspects of social mythology: "One is its genuine aspect, as the body of beliefs or feelings that are held deeply, if often very inarticulately, by a society" (Frye, 1972, p. 16). However, he describes the other aspect of this mythology as "a body of established social principles, to be imposed on everyone without criticism," which pressures all citizens to obey without question, to "adjust" (Frye, 1972, p. 16). He points out, for example, that while American adjustment mythology idealizing cowboys and pioneers may encourage qualities like self-discipline and courage, by its very nature this mythology excludes and marginalizes some segment of the population. According to Frye (1972), "We have no choice about teaching mythology; we have only the choice between teaching genuine and perverted kinds of it" (p. 17). He cautioned that, "this kind of education is formed far more expertly by advertising, especially television commercials. Advertising, being a socially approved form of drug culture, envelops us in an imaginary world, promises us magical powers within that world enabling us to transcend the world we actually live in" (Frye, 1972, p. 17). He points out that advertisers and propagandists are "armed with far more skill, authority, and prestige than any teacher has" (Frye, 1972, p. 18).

7.6 Uncritical Choice-Making

If Frye had concerns about this in 1972, he would be sickened to see to what extent a "perverted" social mythology is pushed at American youth, and how ill-prepared they are to choose willfully to question it. For Frye, the only solution is to teach students "the extent to which they are being conditioned by the mass media" (Frye, 1972, p. 18). He eschewed the idea of treating middle and high school students as if they were incapable of discussing topics like sex or religion intelligently. If the nation's youth are not to be entrapped hopelessly in the endless loop of propagandized narrative meant to circumvent their own cognitive abilities, the only hope is to teach them exactly how narrative is used to merge reason and value—to teach them that repeated stories have the potential to strengthen a sense of community, but also to perpetuate groupthink to the detriment of all. Those excluded and marginalized would not be the only ones to suffer; those unable to own the constructed nature of the truths encoded in the stories would also be trapped, unable to liberate themselves from a false, oversimplified, and very restrictive version of "reality." For example, how would a young woman be able to choose, if she so desired, an alternative to marriage and childbearing if she were unable to see the stereotypic romance narrative as constructed deliberately to not only encourage procreation and the survival of a community, but also to control her options and to limit her journey toward self-actualization? How would an individual from the LGBT community be able to imagine him or herself in this romance narrative? Without the ability to question the stereotypic narrative of the war hero, how would a young man unwilling to fight an unjust war be able to find the courage or the words to explain to his parents that being a conscientious objector does not make him a coward? Throughout human history, there have always been individuals strong and independent enough to resist the social mythology grand narratives propagate. However, in many societies, these individuals have been ostracized or punished cruelly. Beyond this, governments or social mythologies that are undemocratic, intolerant, and unjust undeniably diminish all private and civic life.

In *Women, Fire, and Dangerous Things,* Lakoff (1987) explains how concepts are arranged in the human mind in categories derived from prototypes that work as place markers for cognitive processes (p. 43). For example, the word "criminal" evokes automatically an entire list of stored mental associations in the mind. When subjects are asked to identify the key features of a category, they typically go for the most basic or the most obvious, as opposed to the more subtle distinctions between features (e.g., red as opposed to scarlet). Without prompting, subjects would not consider the many shades of red, but would instead opt for the most obvious, easiest to recall features of the prototypical category color. According to Lakoff (1987), students are programmed cognitively to go for the "central prototype" when identifying a cause/effect relationship. Lakoff (1987) writes that the concept of causation is "used spontaneously, automatically, effortlessly, and often" (p. 55).

Lakoff (1987) points out that advertisers exploit this:

> Since social stereotypes are commonly used to characterize cultural expectations, they tend to be exploited in advertising and in most forms of popular entertainment... An enormous amount of our knowledge about categories of things is organized in terms of typical cases. We constantly draw inferences on the basis of that kind of knowledge. And we do it so regularly and automatically that we are rarely aware that we are doing it. (pp. 85-86)

Further, Lakoff (1987) points out, "we also comprehend categories in terms of individual members who represent either an ideal or its opposite" (p. 87). While "objectivism assumes that correctness is independent of the state of people's minds" (Lakoff, 1987, p. 164), an awareness of how narrative is used to create meaning and of how it leads to stereotyping and oversimplification is necessary for an individual seeking to recognize the important differences between "verisimilitude" and "verification."

If we do not know we are wired to create worlds as opposed to merely perceiving them, we will believe that our worlds actually are as we perceive them; we will be imprisoned by the false absolutes of our own social constructions. If we do not know that there are options for choice, how can we begin to contemplate how best to exercise them? Perry's (1970) often-cited work *Forms of Intellectual Development in the College Years: A Scheme* offers a description of the progression of thought and critical thinking during the college years. Perry developed six levels of critical thought, beginning with level 1—right vs. wrong, or either/or thinking— through level 4, where everyone is entitled to an opinion, to level 6, where ill-structured problems do not have one "right" solution and there are no absolutes, yet action is still necessary. Several theorists and researchers have followed Perry with modifications to the original model. However the model is modified, these progressive levels of critical thinking parallel the type of cognitive development discussed in Blatner's psychological theory. Ultimately, effective thinkers must realize that with more or better information, they might be able to make better choices. Then again, with conscious acceptance of knowledge and time constraints, ethical, effective choices must still be made. The best an individual can do is to compile the best information possible, keeping in mind the impact of choices on the varying stakeholders involved. Perry (1970) describes the evolution of student thought as follows:

> The most difficult instructional moment for the students—and perhaps therefore for the teacher as well—seems to occur at the transition from the conception of knowledge as a quantitative accretion of discrete rightnesses (including the discrete rightnesses of Multiplicity in which everyone has a right to his own opinion) to the conception of knowledge as the qualitative assessment of contextual observations and relationships. (p. 210)

To some degree, Perry's model on the evolution of critical thinking also parallels Paulo Freire's model described in *Pedagogy of the Oppressed* (originally published in 1970), where students move from the "banking concept of education" to an empowerment acquired gradually as they begin to see how capitalism and other oppressive social and political structures limit their choices and options, requiring them to become oppressors themselves and to adopt their oppressors' assumptions and methods in order to achieve economic success. Whatever model is used to explore the movement of an individual mind from repressed, oversimplified absolutism to the acceptance of the subjective nature of human value and knowledge, it seems obvious that people do not learn to traverse this territory on their own. It must be taught, and in the current educational climate—where conversations seem to center on limited resources, standard curricula and assessments, as well as dual enrollment and online options for expeditious movement toward some sort of employment credential—it seems less and less likely that the average American, especially one living in poverty, would be able to acquire the cognitive skills and habits necessary to make the journey without direction and guidance.

7.7 Teaching People to Choose Wisely

How likely is it that the existing corporate, political, and civic institutions perpetuating our current social mythology would make a willing shift toward empowering the undereducated toward capability in unpacking the omnipresent propaganda? One might argue, though it is unlikely that these institutions would listen seriously, that it would make the US more "competitive in a global economy"—a phrase we hear ad nauseam—if we should all accept this as our primary educational goal. Some might argue that the ability to identify nouns in a sentence correctly or to perform algebraic calculations should trump all other educational goals. Certainly, all citizens should be able to read at the targeted Lexile level, but should they also be able to read critically? Many educators would say, "of course." Most educators recognize the importance of the social sciences and the humanities in preparing students to enter the workforce and be effective citizens. One should not assume, however, that educators will always recognize the importance of those competencies, as they are reflective of the democratic values of a particular society in a particular time and place. They, too, are constructed, and so may be deconstructed if enough rhetoric with accompanying narrative is used to justify their irrelevance. Companies want workers who can work both autonomously and collaboratively. They are probably less interested in hiring workers who can choose to organize against them, workers who know how to take action against the current rhetoric of fear, the rhetoric that claims there is not enough, the rhetoric that suggests that those who are concerned about the environment or a living wage are—like Al Gore was branded—"tree-hugging granola heads," or that anyone in the media who attempts to take an independent look at a company or a government institution should simply be labeled "drive-by media" and dismissed. The Horatio Alger myth is still alive and well in the US, as scholars debate the importance of "grit" in the persistence of at-risk students who attempt to complete a high school degree or a college certificate or diploma. It is no accident that the conversation is centered on student "grit" as opposed to all the social and economic factors that impede students, including the heavy debt many acquire in the attempt to achieve a higher level of success.

We need to be able to make the best choices not only as individuals, but as a society. Within our communities, citizens need to first understand the forces preventing the sort of progress they hope to achieve, whether it be peace in a community where racial violence is escalating, or planning for equitable, sustainable use of natural resources. Such choices are possible in a democratic society. While the best information may be difficult to access, it has never been more possible to solve problems, or to improve programs, or to make informed individual choices. At the same time, it has never been more difficult, but that is arguably no accident. Rather, it is the deliberate work of a select few who delude the masses toward false assumption and an increasingly irresistible groupthink. If Thomas Jefferson believed that, given the facts, informed citizens would make the best choices for themselves, their children, and their communities, what would he think of the amount of money spent annually to confuse, frighten, distract, or delude people deliberately into accepting propaganda that erodes at the fabric of our society and ultimately threatens human civilization?

Perhaps it is time for Westerners to learn to look inward for their truths, to clear the mind of the cacophony of competing claims and narratives so that a better, more equitable, and more peaceful way of being can be imagined. If Western society and, indeed, human civilization as a whole, are to recover from the very real threat of global destruction, other narratives beyond the myth of the New Jerusalem, Manifest Destiny, Horatio Alger, Western supremacy, and post-World War II global dominance will have to emerge—social myths of acceptance, tolerance, interdependence, and inclusion. We might start with a healthy respect for some of the basic tenets of Buddhism. After all, the Wheel of Karma identifies greed, hatred/anger, and ignorance perfectly as the root of all human-caused suffering in the world. If we could learn to look deeply into ourselves to encounter the layers of sub-selves—to identify our hidden fears and desires—if we could teach our children to understand that through dialogue we clarify our own understanding and motive—that this is essential before any sort of action should occur—we might be able to teach them to thrive successfully in an uncertain world. If we can teach them to analyze visual and other sorts of rhetoric—especially the narrative frames hidden in TV shows, movies, newspaper and magazine articles and advertisements—they might be less subject to the propaganda and groupthink marketers perpetuate to achieve dominance of the globe for a select few and to the detriment of the entire planet and everything living on it. If we could imagine a society where the endless quest for more power and more material gain is replaced by a quest for harmony and for beauty, we might be able to achieve such a society, or something closer to it. First, we would need the will, the time, and the moral commitment to move together in the right direction. Such movement is all around us every day. If we can examine more closely our motives and our values, perhaps we might choose deliberately to create communities where there is less stress caused by fear. Maybe we could realize together that fewer options might be okay, given that only some options are actually going to sustain our civilization so that all individuals can find it possible to fully self-actualize. Maybe we could let go of pre-emptive war as an option, along with impossibly large houses and the bloat and excess that sicken rather than strengthen. If we could refocus on core democratic and Christian values that will move us ahead in the twenty-first century, we could let go of automatic assumptions and choices that are blindly disastrous. We might see propaganda and delusion for what they are, and liberate ourselves and our children from the hastening alternative path of global destruction.

One final thought: We might better achieve these goals if elite institutions offering graduate degrees in business, marketing, and economics might choose to emphasize sustainability along with best practice models for assessing and implementing business and marketing plans that honor the needs of all stakeholders rather than the ill-founded desires of the insanely greedy few. Perhaps narratives of the futility and psychopathology of narcissistic avarice could be repeated until talented future economists, marketing executives, and MBAs finally understand that wealth is a means to an end, not an end in itself. Maybe then corporate attempts to be ethical would entail more than shallow pitches toward authentic branding aimed at overwhelmed, disillusioned consumers and citizens attempting to determine who best to trust among the most accomplished liars and cheaters in the known universe. If those who enjoy privilege can make an authentic connection between their own well-being and that of undereducated lower-middle class kids with no sense of clear direction, perhaps those who fashion themselves "elites" would more often choose to use their energy, knowledge, and skills to empower everyone in our dying democracy (sometimes called a plutocracy or oligarchy) to the advancement of our society and an improved quality of life for all.

7.8 References

Billig, M. (2013). *Learn to write badly: How to succeed in the social sciences.* Cambridge, England: Cambridge University Press.

Blatner, A. (2002). The implications of postmodern psychotherapy. *Individual Psychology, 53*(4), 476–482. Retrieved from http://www.blatner.com/adam/level2/pmodpsy198.htm

Bruner, J. (1991). The narrative construction of reality. *Critical Inquiry, 18*(1), 1–21.

Chernus, I. (n.d.). Fredric Jameson's interpretation of postmodernism [Webpage]. University of Colorado at Boulder. Retrieved from http://spot.colorado.edu/~chernus/NewspaperColumns/LongerEssays/JamesonPostmodernism.htm

Eggers, D. (2009). *Zeitoun.* San Francisco, CA: McSweeney's Books.

Freire, P. (2009). *Pedagogy of the oppressed.* New York, NY: Continuum International Publishing Group.

Frye, N. (1972). *On teaching literature.* New York, NY: Harcourt, Brace, Jovanovich.

Lakoff, G. (1987). *Women, fire, and dangerous things.* Chicago, IL: University of Chicago Press.

Perry, W. G. (1970). *Forms of intellectual and ethical development in the college years: A scheme.* New York, NY: Holt, Rinehart, & Winston.

Schwartz, B., Ward, A., Monterosso, J., Lyubomirsky, S. White, K., & Lehman, D.R. (2002). Maximizing versus satisficing: Happiness is a matter of choice. *Journal of Personality and Social Psychology, 83*(5), 1178–1197.

Turner, M. (1996). *The literary mind: The origins of thought and language.* Oxford, England: Oxford University Press.

Wright, R. (2005). *Native son.* New York, NY: Harper Perennial Modern Classics.

CHAPTER VIII

A Systematic Solution to Issues of Overchoice and Fairness

Efficient College Course Allocation

Tyler Seacrest

> Most liberal arts colleges and universities now embody a view that celebrates freedom of choice above all else, and the modern university is a kind of intellectual shopping mall . . . . [At Harvard] there are a total of about 220 [general education] courses from which to choose. . . . Princeton offers its students a choice of 350 courses from which to satisfy its general education requirements.
>
> (Schwartz, 2004, p.16)

Following this short vignette piece by Barry Schwartz (2004), it becomes obvious that maximizing individual choice seems to be a desirable pursuit in Western society nowadays. However, maximizing efforts can be hampered by overchoice—the phenomenon of having too many choice options that can support, as well as hinder, the making of efficient and satisfying decisions. In addition, the number of how many choices are available, the variety of choices an assortment has, and the complexity of a decision are major factors that influence the overchoice dynamic.

There is both a positive and negative side to overchoice. The number of choices available to people should help decision-makers. By freeing consumers from monopolistic and profit-oriented shopping constraints, the variety of choices available to consumers should help them have a positive decision-making experience by providing them with autonomy (control) to choose from a manageable assortment of a particular product. While some people benefit from a wealth of choice, others are dissatisfied or suffer. Studies have found that larger choice sets can reduce the quality of a decision (Besedes et al., 2014; Payne, Bettman, & Johnson, 1993), the probability of making a decision (Iyengar & Lepper, 2000; Redelmeier & Shafir, 1995; Roswarski & Murray, 2006), and one's satisfaction with a decision (Iyengar & Lepper, 2000).

One application in which overchoice is noticeable is within multi-unit assignment problems. Some examples of such allocation problems include the assignment of shifts to workers, leads to salespeople, players to sports teams, and airport takeoff and landing slots to airlines. Another example of a multi-unit assignment problem is the efficient allocation of college courses to students. In this case, students want to have the most desirable bundle of courses they can possibly get. As the previous Schwartz excerpt reveals, students can have many course options to choose from, even early on in their college career when they might not have the necessary knowledge to choose the best ones. Ideally, a course allocation system would maximize the positive benefits of choice while minimizing the negative repercussions of overchoice.

In this respect, another property a course allocation system should satisfy is fairness. Because only a limited number of students are permitted to take a given class, students may not get into the classes they desire. Fairness dictates that students should have an equal opportunity to take their desired classes. This further complicates the problem of overchoice. Even if students manage to choose a perfect schedule, they may not be able to take that assortment of classes due to too much demand for certain courses. Some systems, such as auction-based systems, encourage students to use strategies and bids that are not reflective of their true needs and wants. In addition, students who do not know how or do not want to "play the system" are left at a disadvantage.

Increasingly, big institutions use computing power to find a good course match for their students. A handful of these institutions even employ complex software systems with mathematical algorithms to assign students to the best selection of courses possible. Naturally, using such course assignment systems at schools with high enrollments makes sense. However, small institutions deal with the same optimization and allocation issues as their big counterparts, just on a smaller scale. The microcosms of these small entities might not offer the same number of course sections as larger universities, yet they still provide a sizable selection of courses for students.

The following chapter focuses, in part, on exploratory work that employed a course optimization algorithm similar to CourseMatch—used by the University of Pennsylvania—and applied it to a small-school environment. An exploratory experimental design tested and compared this algorithm for matching students with courses to a school's existing course allocation program. Ultimately, while this exploratory work suggested that the algorithm would not be a good match for the targeted school, it identified some areas in which the system could improve course allocation and help alleviate overchoice and unfairness.

This choosing of courses from a great assortment of elective courses is the subject of the following chapter and exploratory research that was conducted in order to present one possible solution to the overchoice dilemma and its affiliated fairness problems.

8.1 Multi-Unit Assignment Problems and Course Allocation

Consider the following scenario: It is late March at a big college. During this particular week, many students are buzzing around campus from building to building and office to office. Contrary to popular belief, it is not mid-term week. Rather, this week is reserved for advising and registration for the coming fall semester. Every student is trying to get the best possible class schedule. Added pressures include the fact that many of these students want to graduate on time, and since the college is a private school, courses are expensive and graduation delays are not welcome. For many of these students, finding the best bundle of courses is quite a challenge since many basic courses offer multiple sections and popular courses fill quickly. So what would be a good solution to make this bi-annual event as fair and as efficient as possible for all the parties involved?

Course allocation is a known problem, and is an example of what economists call the multi-unit assignment problem (Othman, Sandholm, & Budish, 2010). This problem is amplified by the fact that many universities and colleges limit the size of many classes for various reasons (e.g., improve learning outcomes, deal with space issues, support internal politics, create scarcity) (Bartlett 2008). "These class-size limits create an instance of the multi-unit assignment problem [in the realm of overchoice]: if it is not possible for all students to take their most desired schedule of courses, then how should seats in courses be allocated?" (Budish & Cantillon, 2012, p. 2237). Next to course seat allocation problems, multi-unit assignment challenges can also take the form of assignment of shifts or tasks to different workers, players to sports teams, and shared scientific resources to researchers. Budish and Kessler (2015, p. 2) emphasize three reasons that make this situation challenging:

1. The goods are indivisible (e.g., seats in courses).
2. Monetary transfers are prohibited.
3. Agents have preferences defined over bundles of goods (e.g., schedules of courses).

To illustrate why the aforementioned reasons make the situation more challenging from a fairness perspective, consider the following setup in which fifty students want to take a class whose size is capped at twenty-five.

1. If the goods (seats in the class) were divisible, then one could simply allocate each student half a seat in the class. But half a seat in a class does not really make sense. Instead, a subset of the students will enroll in the class, whereas the other students cannot sign up for this class. In the interest of fairness, the other students must be compensated somehow.
1. If monetary transfers were allowed, the unenrolled students could be compensated with money for the loss of utility. However, monetary transfers are often problematic in this setting. Instead, getting an alternative class they value can compensate students who do not get their first choice of class.
2. However, in this case the notion of value is complicated by the fact that students' value bundles of classes rather than individual courses.

> The value of one class may depend on whether a student can get into another class. For example, the value of an algebra class may be solely due to the fact that it is a prerequisite for physics. If a student does not get into the physics class, the algebra course might lose its value.

These three reasons together make the multi-unit assignment problem very challenging. The next section examines more closely what is meant by fairness in the context of college course allocation.

8.2 Fairness Criteria

Fairness has different dimensions and meanings in different disciplines. For the purpose of this chapter, fairness is taken to be a perception of justice of another's advantage; a perception of equity. In the case of course allocation, the literature often discusses that ideal course allocation systems should be envy-free, strategy proof, and efficient (Budish, 2011).

For a division of goods or classes to be envy-free, every student must like their own bundle of goods at least as much as any other student. For students, this means that they can look at the schedules of all the other students without ever wanting to switch schedules with any other students. Note that the concept of envy-free does not capture the idea of fairness fully, as other factors, such as how important a class is in order to graduate, might warrant consideration. However, it is a valuable general criterion that has been employed in many different contexts.

Another fairness criterion is strategy-proof. Often, in order to decide how to divide goods, students should report their preferences so that the best possible division can be undertaken. If a student can get a better bundle of goods by being deceptive and providing false information about his/her preferences, the student is said to be using a strategy. For example, Erin might pretend that getting into course A is of utmost importance to her when in reality she only prefers course A to some extent. In this case, being strategy-proof is useful since it prevents students from "having to engage in costly and risky strategic behavior" (Roth, 2009, p. 79). Strategy-proof systems have some important applications in markets in which, for example, one selects a school to attend, bids in an auction, or searches for a replacement organ (Roth, 2009).

One system that is envy-free and strategy proof is if no student receives any classes. This would be a very undesirable situation. Therefore, a division of goods should satisfy another criterion called efficiency (sometimes called Pareto efficiency). A course allocation system fulfills the requirement for being efficient if there is no possibility to make anyone better off without making someone else worse off. However, in reality, many course allocation mechanisms assign classes in a way that attempts to maximize someone's bundle of courses (making him/her better off) while minimizing someone else's limited course selection (making him/her worse off).

In general, the best allocation system is one that is envy-free, strategy-proof, and efficient. But is this a possible scenario? The answer is that there is no perfect solution. For example, note that no system can be perfectly envy-free. Consider the situation where everyone wants to take one particular star instructor and all other classes are not really desired. In this case, no matter how courses are allocated, the students who do not get the star instructor will envy the students that do. However, even if the envy-freeness condition is greatly weakened, there is no system that is fair, strategy-proof, and efficient (Ehlers & Klaus, 2003; Klaus & Miyagawa, 2001; Pápai, 2001). Therefore, any solution on paper would have to be a compromise to the aforementioned ideal situation. Industry practitioners were also unable to find a viable solution; course-allocation systems that are in use at this time are prone to be inefficient, not tamper-proof, and imbalanced (Sönmez & Ünver, 2010).

Therefore, what possibilities are available to make the existing course assignment systems more envy-free, strategy-proof, and efficient? The upcoming paragraphs examine some approaches that might provide solutions to this problem.

8.3 Types of Course Allocation Systems

Finding the right courses can be a stressful process for students, advisors, and—last but not least—the registrar's office. Following are some approaches—such as first-come, first-served systems, auctions with multiple rounds, draft systems, and one-round equilibrium assignment systems—that might provide solutions to the aforementioned problem.

A. First-Come, First-Served

The simplest and most widely used course allocation system is first-come, first-served (Diebold et al., 2014). In this system, each student signs up for classes any time after a certain date. A student can enroll in any class that has seats available. In other words, the earlier a student signs up for classes, the more likely it is that the student gets into the classes he/she wants. This system has two advantages:

1. It is simple, and therefore easy for students to understand and implement.
2. It is fair in the sense that every student has the same chance of getting classes as any other student. If a student fails to get into a course that he/she wanted, it is his/her own fault for not signing up for classes earlier.

However, this sense of fairness can turn into unfairness under certain circumstances. For instance, there may be valid reasons why someone needs to register later than others. Is it fair to disadvantage one student over another based on their availability? Also, it becomes unwieldy if a large group of students tries to enroll at the same time when registration opens. First-come, first-served most certainly violates the principle of envy-freeness. The last students who sign up may be forced to take classes they find less desirable, and might be willing to trade schedules with students who signed up earlier.

B. Auction System

To a certain extent, an auction system can resolve the problems associated with the first-come, first-served approach, especially in the case a lot of students attempt to register at the same time. Colorado College is an example of an institution that uses an auction system (Benson, Johnson, & Lybecker, 2013). In an auction system, every student is provided with an equal amount of fake money to be used for bidding on classes. If a class is capped at 25, than the 25 highest bidders get into this class. This is a fair system in the sense that every student receives the same amount of money, and therefore has an equal opportunity to enroll in the classes they want.

However, this system is not strategy-proof. Knowing how things might develop is of great strategic importance to a student registering through an auction system. Furthermore, there might be an inequity among bidders as far as having information and willingness to strategize is concerned, and hence it is not envy-free. Having multiple rounds in the auction reduces this problem. With multiple rounds, all bidders have increased access to information and details about previous rounds. However, that might be a reason why a student should not reveal what their auction strategy is until the final round in an effort to lower the price. A multi-round auction requires a great deal of organization by school officials and commitment by students.

C. Draft System

An example of the draft system that has been in place since the 1990s is a course allocation system utilized by Harvard Business School (Budish & Cantillon, 2012). The Harvard Business School draft asks students to plug their course preferences into a computer. In the first round, the computer chooses one class after another for each student in random order. In later rounds, the computer chooses more classes for the students, but the order of the selection process is reversed. Students are assigned courses one at a time, based on their preferences they plugged into the computer earlier and available seats in the respective courses.

Such a system is envy-free and efficient to a high degree. However, it is not strategy-proof. A student, for example, might use the first round to draft not their most preferred class, but a class they want and that they think will be popular, thus using their course seat as leverage to bargain. This is not just a theoretical problem, but occurs in practice as well (Budish & Cantillon, 2012). Other deficiencies of this system are logistical implementation issues which can occur in any system that uses multiple iterations to generate a solution.

D. Competitive Equilibrium from Equal Incomes

The method this research employs is called competitive equilibrium from equal incomes (CEEI). Budish (2011) proposed this mechanism, which he derived from the old general equilibrium theory approach of competitive equilibrium from equal incomes by Foley (1967) and Varian (1974). This mechanism seems to have a high degree of equity and only requires one round of choosing. Like the draft system, students plug their preferences for courses into a computer, and then the computer calculates the best bundle of classes for the student. The Wharton Business School at the University of Pennsylvania is currently testing this approach of allocating courses.

The CEEI is an auction-based system that starts with the student's preferences. The preferences are a rating for each class that tells the computer how much that student wants that class. Like the auction system, CEEI assigns a specific amount of fake money to each student and a price to each class. Given prices for each class, the computer determines which courses a student bets on; hopefully, the classes that maximize the given preferences are also a set of classes the student can afford. If the prices are acceptable and the preferences are accurate, this is the best possible schedule for the student given these prices.

The prices for each course are set exactly at a level where no class is bought by too many students, and every class with a nonzero price is full. This is called the market-clearing price. It is an efficient system because if one student did not get into a preferred class, that means the class was full and another student would have to be unenrolled to make the first student better off. It is efficient as long as a student does not bid on classes that he/she could have gotten for free.

It should be mentioned that the bids the computer makes for the student are different from their preferences. Suppose Erin indicates that her highest ranked class is a political science class and places a score of 100 on it, while she ranks a sociology class at little bit lower (but still fairly high) and places a score of 75 on it. If there is little demand for the political science class, the computer will bid nothing or very little on the political science class despite its high score, because the computer system is aware of the fact that Erin can get into the class by only spending a small amount of fake money. This, in return, would enable Erin to spend the saved money on classes that she also prefers, but that have a higher clearing price.

There is no reason to enter fake preferences to gain a strategic advantage. The computer is already using the best possible strategy, and skewing preferences will result in the computer applying an inefficient strategy. Therefore, CEEI is strategy-proof. However, in the greater scheme of things, this is a slight oversimplification. Budish (2011) proves that the CEEI is strategy-proof for large markets, but may not be under all circumstances.

CEEI is not envy-free, but it is approximately envy-free. More precisely, the envy of CEEI is tied to a single class. What does this mean? Imagine Erin can sign up for classes W, X, Y, and Z, while David can sign up for classes A, B, and C, and that David envies Erin's class selection. Then, if in fact envy is tied to a single good, then while David envies the selection {W, X, Y, Z}, he does not envy the selection {W, X, Y}. That is, if a single class is removed from this bundle, the envy disappears.

Thus, the CEEI is efficient and strategy-proof, and envy is tied to a single class. It is also potentially a tool to help overcome the negative aspects of overchoice. Furthermore, it is a single-round system in which the computer does most of the work. These attributes seem to make the CEEI the most preferred course allocation system.

CEEI is currently being tested at Wharton Business School under the name "Course Match," replacing an auction-based system. Budish and Kessler (2015) find that the CEEI has been a considerable improvement over the auction system, a fact which generated very positive responses from users of CEEI.

Following is a discussion of the research design that tested the CEEI in a small-campus environment.

8.4 Research Design

A. Research Problem

The aim of this effort was to investigate whether the CEEI course allocation system can provide some benefit over the first-come, first-served system—in terms of fairness and managing overchoice—at a small institution that uses a modular scheduling system rather than semester-long classes.

In the modular scheduling system, students take one course at a time over a period of four weeks. During a semester, students take four courses, one after the other. The school has approximately 1000 students taking a modular class during any given month, and offers approximately 50 classes per timeframe capped at 25 students per class, providing a slight oversupply of classes. The level of course excess-capacity in this modular scheduling system corresponds roughly to a single semester course allocation problem at an average school.

B. Experimental Design

The exploratory design placed groups of participants (students) into a market for the school's courses in a hypothetical semester. In the face of scarcity and competition from others, subjects were asked to construct the best schedule of four courses that they could design, first under the school's existing course allocation system (first-come, first served), and then under the new mechanism (CEEI). Under each mechanism, subjects were instructed to "construct their most preferred schedule of general education courses" from the course sections available in 2014-2015 course catalog.

Participants were asked to construct a schedule under the first mechanism. Respondents then constructed a schedule under the second mechanism, starting from scratch (i.e., starting with zero courses, just as in the first mechanism). After using each mechanism, participants answered survey questions about the mechanism and the schedule they received. After using both mechanisms, respondents were asked to select which of the two mechanisms they prefer by answering additional survey questions about both mechanisms and writing free-response comments.

C. The Sample

The school examined has a population of a little bit over 1000 students. A group of 71 students participated in this exploratory research. The participants were selected through convenient sampling. Convenience sampling was determined to be the most viable sampling option at this exploratory research stage. The participants completed the schedules and questionnaires in a computer lab on campus.

D. The Research Instrument

The system that the school, which is located in the West, uses to select courses involves a fairly common course-allocation approach that is based on a first-come, first-served system. It combines working out a schedule on paper, conferring with a student advisor, and then enrolling in the classes online by considering availability. Course allocation for the following semester usually takes place in the middle of the previous semester. To make the school's existing system simple enough to play during the experimental session, the study used a simplified version of the system for the experiment. The version considered only general education classes that can fulfill the required general education core curriculum (there were eight general-education course groups students could choose from). This approach was used to have classes of the same level to which students have equal access, regardless of their academic standing (freshman, sophomore, junior, or senior). The instructions for the existing system were relatively familiar to most participants, since many of them had used the system before to select their courses. Respondents used a standard web interface similar to the real system so that the process would be as familiar as possible.

After the students used the first system, they were instructed on how to use the second system, which is based on CEEI. Following are the three steps that were used for the second system.

1. Each participant reports his/her preference by rating each class he/she has at least some interest in taking (The research instructions recommended that a student allocates 100 points to his/her most preferred course and then give points to other courses in proportion).
2. The computer finds (approximate) market-clearing prices.
3. Each respondent is allocated the most preferred and affordable bundle of classes—the affordable bundle the student likes best given the preferences in step (1) and given he/she can afford it based on the amount of fake money he/she receives and the prices found in step (2).

The questions were rated on the following seven-point Likert scale: 1="Strongly Disagree," 2="Disagree," 3= "Somewhat Disagree," 4="Neither Agree or Disagree," 5="Somewhat Agree," 6="Agree," 7="Strongly Agree." The overall mean scores for the old system (based on first-come, first-served) and the new system (based on CEEI) are computed from the response values across all participants. Higher average numbers indicate higher agreement with the statement.

8.5 Results

The goal of the new system was to optimize the allocation of seats (ensuring the best possible class schedule for each student), eliminate the incentive to strategize and the worry that others can gain an advantage through strategic play, and require only a single round of course-search per semester. However, some unique challenges emerged in this smaller setting.

After the subjects used each course allocation mechanism, they answered questions using a ranking scale about the schedule they received and the mechanism they had just used. These questions addressed the simplicity and clarity of the course allocation mechanism, general liking of the mechanisms, and the strategic effort required to use them. After the subjects used both mechanisms, they answered additional questions, including one free response question in which students listed why they preferred the system they did.

The free response question painted a similar picture as the questions that used a ranking scale. The majority of the written responses indicate that the old first-come, first-served system seemed to be more convenient, and envy-free to a high degree. In a lot of answers the presence (combination) of the small, personable environment and a not too overwhelming number of general education choices are mentioned as factors that contribute to this preference.

As the outcomes of this exploratory study suggest, the CEEI system seems to have difficulty functioning as intended in small school environments. As the results indicate, the existing system in small environments does not produce sufficient envy in order for the CEEI system to be seen as an improvement; subjects appear to perceive the existing small-campus system as fair enough.

In theory, the first-come, first-served method gives every student an equal opportunity to enroll in the classes they want, and is therefore fair. Students who register earlier in this system get a better schedule than those who register later. However, the notion of fairness in this system can be skewed if students register late for reasons not under their control, or if a considerable number of students sign up exactly at the same time when registration starts. The initial findings show that this does not occur at the institution under examination. No student in the free response answers indicated any major problems getting into the classes they wanted. Students who signed up at or near the start date reported getting into all the classes they desired. Some students liked the fact that the first-come, first-served approach rewards students for being organized and signing up for classes early.

The reason why the first-come, first-served structure is working well at this institution seemed to be a lack of scarcity. While the research has not collected any specific data on the level of competition for classes, it is speculated that most students get into the classes they want most of the time. In case a student cannot enroll into a class they want, they have other viable classes to choose from. As a result, there is little pressure to sign up at or near the start date, which results in low enrollment at the beginning. Those who do sign up at the beginning are practically ensured of getting their most preferred schedule.

No student addressed the fact that first-come, first-served is not envy-free. However, there was a small, but significant, minority of students who said they preferred CEEI. The most common reason was that the simulated CEEI system assigned them their most preferred schedule. However, many also mentioned that they felt the CEEI was fairer, even if they did not address the concept of envy-freeness specifically.

Another major theme of the responses was the desire for seniors to have a higher priority than juniors, sophomores, and freshmen when accessing classes. In the first-come, first-served course allocation system, seniors can sign up a day before juniors, who can sign up a day before sophomores, who can sign up a day before freshman. Several students mentioned this as the primary reason they preferred first-come, first-served.

Some assumptions were made as to what conditions might have to be in place in order for the CEEI system to work in smaller settings:

- Scarcity of (elective) classes.
- An easy to use online class selection system.
- A mechanism to help those nearing graduation receive the classes they need.
- The administration's willingness to encourage ownership of the students in their class registration.
- The students' willingness to be proactive stakeholders in the class selection process.
- A school that favors educational entrepreneurship and is ready to try something innovative and new.

The following paragraphs discuss the results of this research effort.

8.6 Discussion of Results

Even though the results were not very clear, overall, students were more satisfied with their CEEI schedules than with those generated by the old system (at specific large institutions). They were less envious of their peers' schedules, and they found the new system easier to use, even though they received only minimal training on the new system (CEEI-based system). Another interesting element of the present study was that the participants used the same complex choices they had to make in the first-come, first-served system (auction system) for the CEEI-based system, but were able to enter them more conveniently. Thus, CEEI represents a new kind of market design success story with course allocation at bigger schools. However, this current research suggests that the same market design can face unique challenges at smaller schools and outside the semester system.

As with all studies, this research was confined by some limitations. The sample size was rather small, hence the exploratory nature of the study. Future versions of this study have to do a better job of using a more appealing frontend of the user interface to encourage more realistic data entry for courses. The study focused only on general education courses which were equally accessible to all students. Some of the students that participated in the study indicated that the new allocation algorithm is too much of an enclosed system that lacks transparency. Given these limitations, the following opportunities for future editions of the study can be suggested: A bigger sample can be used by including not only institutions that operate in a modular system, but also institutions that operate in a modular system; future studies can expand on the existing research and examine how different genders and different majors choose courses; and future studies also have to look beyond general education classes and include major-specific courses in their assortment options.

Overall, and mostly at large institutions, the new system optimizes the allocation of seats (ensuring the best possible class schedule for each student), eliminates the incentive to strategize and the worry that others can gain an advantage through strategic play, and requires only a single round of course search per semester. The main results of this exploratory effort conclude that the system can manage overchoice and optimize course allocation conveniently at large institutions, but faces some unique challenges at smaller institutions, which future research might be able to resolve.

8.7 Future Opportunities: Expanding the System

Based on the previous work, the most pressing issue regarding fairness is to ensure students get the classes they need in order to graduate on time. An example of this would be a senior who just needs one or two specific classes to graduate. Another example might be a freshman math major who needs to get into a trigonometry class in their first year in order to be able take all other classes in the math major and complete his/her studies in four years.

Adding a mechanism to the CEEI-based system that would give first priority to students who need a course to graduate is recommended. This mechanism could have the following form:

1. All students, as soon as they are able to, would enter their major and expected graduation date into the system.
2. Before course registration starts, the computer would use an algorithm to identify the classes they need in order to graduate on time, in essence generating a degree audit. (For the purpose of this discussion, these classes will be called high-priority classes).
3. While students report on their preferences, the computer will alert them of the classes that qualify as high-priority. They would then have the choice of checking a box that indicates an interest in signing up for the high-priority classes. Students can also petition school officials to get a class counted as high-priority if they think the computer has made an error.
4. Then, the CEEI system uses a two-round course allocation. During the first round, all high-priority classes are assigned. During the second round, all other classes are assigned using the remaining seats.

Step four ensures that no student who needs a class to graduate is bumped in favor of a student who does not need the class. In fact, everyone who needs a class to graduate will get into that class, except in the unlikely event that there are more people who need that class to graduate than there are spaces available in the course.

It might be a considerable challenge to construct a mathematical algorithm to determine if a class is necessary to graduate. It would require that the computer knows which courses are necessary for each major, all the course rotations for the required classes, and which courses are prerequisites for others. Provided the computer has this information, this system could be put in place. However, the course rotation piece poses a particular challenge, since this rotation is often updated and changed due to enrollment dynamics and labor market needs. A way to alleviate this pressure on the system would be if the system could only automatically flag classes as high-priority if they appear in the last year for a graduating senior.

If implemented, this system may be expanded easily to give students recommendations on how to report their class preferences. This system could provide students with considerable benefits early on in their academic career, especially those who find a large number of choices paralyzing, and who lack an understanding of how their major is structured.

8.8 References

Bartlett, T. (2008, February 15). Class warfare: When getting in is the hardest part. *The Chronicle of Higher Education.* Retrieved from http://chronicle.com/article/Class-Warfare-When-Getting-In/13092

Benson, C., Johnson, D. K. N., & Lybecker, K. M. (2013). *Bidding for classes: Course allocation under the Colorado college auction system.* Colorado College Working Paper No 2013-2. Retrieved from http://ssrn.com/abstract=2257921

Besedes, T., Deck, C. A., Sarangi, S., & Shor, M. (2014). *Reducing choice overload without reducing choices.* Netspar Discussion Paper No. 09/2012-064. Retrieved from http://papers.ssrn.com/sol3/papers.cfm?abstract_id=2357376

Budish, E. (2011). The combinatorial assignment problem: Approximate competitive equilibrium from equal incomes. *Journal of Political Economy, 119*(6), 1061–1103.

Budish, E., & Cantillon, E. (2012). The multi-unit assignment problem: Theory and evidence from course allocation at Harvard. *American Economic Review, 102*(5), 2237–2271.

Budish, E., & Kessler, J. (2015). *Experiments as a bridge from market design theory to market design practice: Changing the course allocation mechanism at Wharton.* Working Paper. Retrieved from http://citeseerx.ist.psu.edu/viewdoc/download?doi=10.1.1.720.855&rep=rep1&type=pdf

Diebold, F., Bichler, M., Matthes, F., Schneider, A. W., & Aziz, H. (2014). Course allocation via stable matching. *Business & Information Systems Engineering, 6*(2), 97–110.

Ehlers, L., & Klaus, B. (2003). Coalitional strategy-proof and resource-monotonic solutions for multiple assignment problems. *Social Choice and Welfare, 21*(2), 265–280.

Foley, D. K. (1967). Resource allocation and the public sector. *Yale Economic Essays, 7*(1), 45–98.

Iyengar, S. S., & Lepper, M. R. (2000). When choice is demotivating: Can one desire too much of a good thing? *Journal of Personality and Social Psychology, 79*(6), 995–1006.

Klaus, B., & Miyagawa, E. (2001). Strategy-proofness, solidarity, and consistency for multiple assignment problems. *International Journal of Game Theory, 30*(3), 421–435.

Othman, A., Sandholm, T., & Budish, E. (2010). Finding approximate competitive equilibria: Efficient and fair course allocation. *Proceedings of the 9th International Conference on Autonomous Agents and Multiagent Systems* (AAMAS '10), *1*(1), 873–880.

Pápai, S. (2001). Strategyproof and nonbossy multiple assignments. *Journal of Public Economic Theory, 3*(3), 257–271.

Payne, J. W., Bettman, J. R., & Johnson, E. J. (1993). *The adaptive decision maker.* Cambridge, England: Cambridge University Press.

Redelmeier, D. A., & Shafir, E. (1995). Medical decision making in situations that offer multiple alternatives. *Journal of the American Medical Association, 273*(4), 302–305.

Roswarski, T. E., & Murray, M. D. (2006). Supervision of students may protect physicians from cognitive bias: A study of decision making and multiple treatment alternatives in medicine. *Medical Decision Making, 26*(2), 154–161.

Roth, A. (2009). What have we learned from market design? In J. Lerner & S. Stern (Eds.), *Innovation Policy and the Economy* (Vol. 9, pp. 79–112). Chicago, IL: University of Chicago Press.

Sönmez, T., & Ünver, U. (2010). Course bidding at business schools. *International Economic Review, 51*(1), 99–123.

Schwartz, B. (2004). *The paradox of choice: Why more is less.* New York, NY: Harper Collins.

Varian, H. R. (1974). Equity, envy, and efficiency. *Journal of Economic Theory,* 9(1), 63–91.

Index

S

T

U

V

W